In Pursuit of Excellence

The Community College of Denver

5 - 30 - 2006

FOR DAVID —

WITH OUR

BEST WISHES!

John + Suanne

John E. Roueche, Eileen E. Ely, and Suanne D. Roueche

Community College Press®
a division of the American Association of Community Colleges
Washington, D.C.

The American Association of Community Colleges (AACC) is the primary advocacy organization for the nation's community colleges. The association represents 1,100 two-year, associate degree-granting institutions and some 10 million students. AACC provides leadership and service in five key areas: policy initiatives, advocacy, research, education services, and coordination/networking.

Dedication

This book is dedicated to our friend and colleague

Byron McClenney
President
Community College of Denver
(1986–2000)

and

the entire Community College of Denver team

*who lead by example and live the dream of making good
on the promise of the open door.*

Contents

Figures

Tables

Foreword

In Pursuit of Excellence: The Community College of Denver is a story of success, of overcoming the odds by a dedicated faculty, staff, and administration who, together, determined that they were going to make a positive difference for their community and its most disadvantaged people. It is a story of leadership and change.

The book, however, is more than a compelling story; it is a blueprint of how an urban community college with inadequate resources, serving a diverse and increasingly at-risk student body, was able dramatically to improve and document the success of its students. What happened at the Community College of Denver under Byron McClenney's leadership can be a model for transforming other educational institutions.

Suanne and John Roueche, two of higher education's most thoughtful observers and articulate commentators, join with Eileen Ely to examine issues that are at the core of the values of American community colleges. Since their founding 100 years ago, community colleges have provided millions of Americans access to higher education and an opportunity for a better life. However, both the colleges themselves and their extensive remedial education programs have come under periodic criticism. A lack of data on learning outcomes and effectiveness of programs has left the colleges vulnerable to poor public policy decisions.

The authors set the context by examining the historical evolution of open access to higher education in the United States and the consequent development of remedial programs. Demands for accountability led to the establishment of core indicators to measure institutional effectiveness. In particular, community colleges were asked to document student goal attainment, degree completion rates, persistence, and other outcome measures.

The Community College of Denver made a commitment to improve educational outcomes for its students—especially for students of color— and to document their level of success. From the 1986 college convocation that gave birth to this shared commitment, to environmental scans, to studying best practices at other community colleges and establishing benchmarks, to implementing an annual planning process linked to resource allocation, to reorganization of the college, to development of shared values for student learning, and to agreeing on critical skills across the curriculum, the book documents how changes made a difference. The success of the Community College of Denver in dramatically increasing student diversity while virtually eliminating the achievement gap between minority and non-minority students is remarkable. Its successes are widely recognized among community colleges nationwide, and in March 2000, the college received the prestigious Hesburgh Award for the effectiveness of its Teaching/ Learning Center.

Those of us in the community college field owe a debt of gratitude to Byron McClenney and his team at the Community College of Denver for demonstrating that community colleges can lead the way in improving success rates for disadvantaged students and how we can document that success. I sincerely thank Suanne and John Roueche and Eileen Ely for a significant contribution and for inspiring all of us to make good on the promise of America's community colleges.

George R. Boggs
President and CEO
American Association of Community Colleges

Preface

In the 1960s, President Edmund J. Gleazer of the American Association of Community Colleges challenged community colleges to make good on the implied promise of the open door. Today, community colleges continue to reduce barriers to higher education, to allow students from modest means to earn a college degree, and to evolve a curriculum to meet an array of personal, economic, and societal needs. Students are being shunted from higher education because facilities and equipment are so underfunded that colleges cannot meet the demands. And there are steadily increasing numbers of students—those we label at risk of failure—we simply are not reaching or teaching effectively.

The promise of the open door is an invitation for community colleges to serve the entire student population. When we invite all students to our teaching and learning tables, we should plan that their time with us be well spent and that they leave us better than when they began, equipped with knowledge, tools, competencies, and credentials to improve the quality of their lives.

In this report, we did not intend to write about remedial or developmental education. Rather we intended to write about the responses an institution made to academically at-risk students as enthusiastically as it did to any other. We have observed over the years that responding positively to the needs of at-risk students can make colleges more responsive to *all* students. We have witnessed the enormous effects that an institution's caring deeply about the success of those who are most underprepared for college work and least able to contribute to society can have on an entire institution, on its community, and on the nation.

We have watched the Community College of Denver (CCD) taking measured steps of progress for more than a decade. The college's efforts to level the educational playing field have been documented well and have received national recognition and acclaim—rightly so, as the results are simply astounding.

We are thankful for the support of so many CCD professionals without whose help and information we could not have accurately reported the college's progress and success. Byron McClenney, CCD president from 1986 to summer 2000, led the faculty and staff to its proud achievements—valuing diversity, securing second chance opportunities, and keeping open door promises by commitment and example for all students. We extend a special thank you to President McClenney for allowing us to experience the college's pursuit of excellence in person on so many occasions.

We have many others to thank for their timely and thoughtful responses to our requests for details and documentation. We enjoyed experiencing their passion for CCD and their vision of its future. We are indebted especially to:

- Barbara Bollman, Vice President, Instruction
- Greg Smith, Vice President, Information, Research, and Planning
- Janet White-Butler, Director, Academic Support Center
- Dianne Cyr, Dean, Center for Learning Outreach
- Levi Crespin, Dean, Center for Educational Advancement
- Peggy Valedez-Fergason, Director, La Familia Scholars Program
- Patricia Jensen, Director, Institutional Advancement
- Wanda Underwood, Executive Assistant, President's Office
- Developmental Education program coordinators, faculty, and support services staff, Center for Educational Advancement and the Technical Education Centers
- Orlando Griego, retired, former Dean, Center for Education and Academic Services (now called the Center for Educational Advancement)
- Yvonne Frye, Professor, English, Summer Bridge Program
- Darilyn Carroll, Coordinator, Service Learning Program
- Ann Johnson, retired, former Coordinator, Education, English, and GED Programs; currently Faculty Emeritus
- John Robey, Assistant to the VP of Instruction
- Clare Lewis, Administrative Assistant, Teaching and Learning Center

Here at the University of Texas at Austin, we thank Sheryl Fielder Powell for her contributions to yet another major writing project. For more than a decade, she has brought a keen editor's eye to our manuscripts and organization to our thinking; has tended to the last-minute, exhaustive publication guidelines and the dreaded bibliography checks; and has helped deliver our message better than we could have done it alone. She does not know the depths of her enormous talent!

The two of us who live and work in Austin, Texas, congratulate and thank again our co-author who lives and works in Riverton, Wyoming. She was as involved throughout this project as though she were sitting at the next desk in the same room. Throughout the writing process, the three of us were never farther away than an e-mail and a fax. We developed a deeper appreciation for the technology and enjoyed the unique collaborative experience immensely.

Finally, the three of us tip our Texas and Wyoming hats to our Colorado friends and colleagues who are living out their dream of making good on the promise of the open door at the Community College of Denver. We appreciate the opportunity to tell their extraordinary story.

John E. Roueche
Eileen E. Ely
Suanne D. Roueche

Golden Goals and Rusted Realities: Where Are We Now?

A disturbing and dangerous mismatch exists between what American society needs of higher education and what it is receiving. Nowhere is the mismatch more dangerous than in the quality of undergraduate preparation provided on many campuses. The American imperative for the twenty-first century is that society must hold higher education to much higher expectations or risk national decline. — **Wingspread Group on Higher Education 1993**

No one could ever accuse community colleges of having lackluster goals. Community colleges are dedicated to serving and developing their communities, to improving America's workforce, and to encouraging lifelong learning—but above all, to being the pathway to a better life for their students, taking them from where and how they are when they matriculate to where they want to go. Without a doubt, these are laudable, golden goals. They set community colleges apart from other institutions of higher education and show our priorities. We are, first and foremost, teaching institutions and colleges of learning.

But these goals are rarely achieved with such success that the efforts and their results generate serious study. While recent research shows that the public's opinion of community colleges is improving, at the same time there is a growing mistrust of and exasperation with higher education in general—its cost, its focus, and—in particular—its quality.

GAUGING INSTITUTIONAL EFFECTIVENESS FOUR YEARS AGO

Colleges often find themselves unable to prove their effectiveness as educational institutions. When comparing the results with their stated goals, colleges may discover they come up short. Community colleges are challenged to meet the goals they have set in their mission statements and to prove to a diverse mix of critics and judges—students and communities—that their performance matches their stated purpose.

Our 1997 study of institutional effectiveness, *Embracing the Tiger: The Effectiveness Debate and the Community College* (Roueche, Johnson, and Roueche), documented that colleges in general were taking slow but significant steps to demonstrate their effectiveness. Most colleges were responding primarily to pressure from external sources—accrediting agencies and funding entities—and boards of trustees, rather than to faculty or administrative demands for more accountability. We found only one college in five had adopted practices to ask more questions and gather more performance data than required by outside forces.

From survey responses and anecdotal information, we also determined the majority of colleges were not collecting data that would tell them, in fact, if they were fulfilling their mission: This finding runs contrary to the body of literature regarding institutional effectiveness. We concluded colleges did not understand how to link mission to effectiveness measures, were not inclined to do so, or had not thought of it. They were, primarily, reporting their performance on the more traditional indicators of effectiveness—i.e., degree and completion rates, growth, cost containment, diversity, and transfer rates.

Learning-related indicators did not receive the attention that we anticipated. The only exceptions were in the Southern and North Central Association's accrediting regions where assessment of student academic achievement is a major issue. Public dissatisfaction with higher education can only be quieted by colleges compiling data beyond transfer rates. It is incumbent on colleges to gauge industry's and the community's satisfaction with graduates: by assessing programs and services; by documenting the success of developmental programs; and, most important, by determining how students exiting developmental courses performed in subsequent college-level courses. The interest in articulating core indicators for institutional—read student—success was serious and strong.

Our research unearthed one excellent model of indicators. This model, developed by the Community College Roundtable and published as

Community Colleges: Core Indicators of Effectiveness (1994), addressed the need for "models to use in assessing effectiveness that are unique to the community college and that would reflect core measures *implicit in its mission*" (4, emphasis added). Most important, the roundtable members emphasized that these core indicators not only *should* be measured, they *must* be measured, and they should describe "the major mission tasks that a community college must accomplish to be successful" (6). Figure 1.1 shows the model as updated for the second edition of the report, *Core Indicators of Effectiveness for Community Colleges* (Alfred et al. 1999).

For each indicator in the model there are measures and potential sources of data. Indicators include the following:

- Student goal attainment
- Persistence (fall to fall)
- Degree completion rates
- Placement rate in the workforce
- Employer assessment of students
- Licensure certification/pass rates
- Client assessment of programs and services
- Demonstration of critical literacy skills
- Demonstration of citizenship skills
- Number and rate who transfer
- Performance after transfer
- Success in subsequent, related course work
- Participation rate in service area
- Responsiveness to community needs

The core indicators combine internal and external perspectives on a common theme—student success. By design, the roundtable paper did not address other indicators that members agreed were important considerations to measure institutional effectiveness comprehensively—e.g., resource allocation and staff development. Rather, members chose to focus on student success as central to the college's mission.

We concluded our institutional effectiveness study with a number of recommendations, including that colleges begin, with expediency, to measure institutional effectiveness in a timely and appropriate manner, adapt the successful practices of others to fit their own situations, involve individuals who will be affected most by the effectiveness measures in planning and discussion, join with other community colleges to agree in principle on the

Figure 1.1 Core Indicators of Institutional Effectiveness

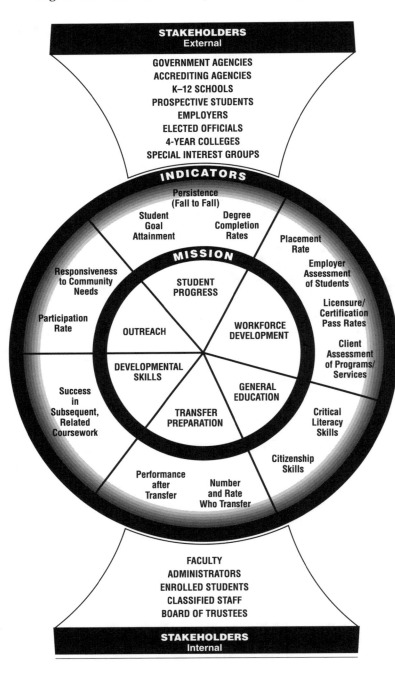

major criteria by which they all should be judged, and establish consequences for poor performance to prevent loss of credibility.

GAUGING INSTITUTIONAL EFFECTIVENESS TODAY

As predicted by researchers, institutional effectiveness issues have received more attention, funding has gone down, and college budgets have shrunk. Yet there are more community college success stories to tell than were available just four years ago. Increased awareness and improved data collection appear to indicate that colleges are more sensitive to the important step of tying their mission statements to their indicators of effectiveness, experimenting with measurement strategies, and fine-tuning the most applicable measures to their own institution.

Progress is progress, albeit slow; and progress expands and clarifies useful models. Every successful college we know of committed hard work and time; there are no "overnight success" stories. But there are extraordinary stories to be told, and the Community College of Denver (CCD) is one.

THE CRITICAL ISSUE OF DEVELOPMENTAL EDUCATION

Perhaps the greatest challenge facing community colleges is appropriate responses to increasingly diverse student populations. The challenges permeate such controversial issues as academic preparation, need, cost, delivery methods, and effectiveness. Arguments about the controversies embroil uneven academic experiences for students of color; the appropriateness of remediation at the higher education level; the real cost to college-level programs when developmental programs draw from the total college budget; and instructional methodologies for remediation and developing basic skills in adult students. Perhaps the most heated dispute is whether remedial education is worth the time, effort, and money to the student, the college, and society. Controversy aside, one fact remains clear: More than 50 percent of all first-time students in community colleges need remedial or developmental work in one or more basic skill areas before enrolling in college-level courses (McCabe and Day 1998). Otherwise their chances for academic success are poor and none. There can be no argument that these controversial issues must be addressed.

Critics contend that the funds spent on remediation outweigh the gain and skill-deficient students have had their chances, so students receiving remedial services should pay for it (McCabe and Day 1998). Proponents argue that developmental education is essential to maintaining democratic access to higher education. Philosophically, proponents believe that the open-door concept—or universal access to college—is the essential ingredient to maintaining democracy and to improving the quality of life and to bettering our society (McCabe and Day 1998; Roueche 1968). William Brock, chair of the 1993 Wingspread Group on Higher Education, warned: "An increasingly open, global economy requires—absolutely requires—that all of us be better educated, more skilled, or adaptable, and more capable of working collaboratively" (1993, 5). Developmental education is charged with producing knowledgeable adults and a skilled workforce.

Senior institutions have insisted that remedial course work has no place in a college curriculum; yet they lament the consequent decreases in enrollment, campus diversity, and loss of revenue that are the direct results of acting on their opinions. While community colleges are willing to tackle this growing challenge, they worry about the effects of increased demands on already tight budgets, with anticipated future reductions in funding. The increased cost of ever-larger numbers of academically under-prepared students could ultimately affect their transfer and occupational functions (Ignash 1997). Others fear they will turn community colleges into "educational emergency-care clinics" (Raisman 1994, 25).

Many federal and state legislators and higher education systems, frustrated with underprepared freshman students, are implementing an array of policies restricting postsecondary developmental education. In addition to designating community colleges as preferred developmental education providers, mandates have been recommended to limit remediation to the freshman year, to restrict the number of remedial courses offered, to eliminate financial aid funds to skill-deficient students, and to require public school systems to reimburse colleges for the costs of remediating basic skills of public school graduates (National Center for Education Statistics [hereafter referred to as NCES] 1996).

Many policymakers believe that most developmental education students are recent high school graduates, but the demographics of today's developmental programs mirror the changing demographics in America. There are increasing numbers of single parents, high school dropouts (or even dropouts from elementary and middle schools), workers in training and/or retraining, and new immigrants. Data show no slackening of these trends.

The current workforce is undereducated. Recent figures indicate that more than one-fourth of American workforce are functionally illiterate (McCabe and Day 1998). The crisis of illiteracy is monumental with the shifting of labor skills in the technological era. Today only about 20 percent of all employees are working at manual tasks. "Of the remainder, nearly half, 40 percent of our total workforce, are knowledge workers" (Drucker 2000, 86).

Current research on remedial and developmental education urges colleges to develop more comprehensive developmental education plans to address current and future skill-deficient students. Not only will viable plans help colleges better serve their communities and improve the quality of the nation's workforce, but they can also help develop a significant revenue stream for the college.

With for-profit institutions willing to provide basic skills training, community colleges must not only embrace developmental education, but work collaboratively with K–12 schools and traditional colleges and universities to develop strategies for success. Furthermore, to appease external constituents, including legislators and accrediting agencies, community colleges must be able to accurately evaluate program effectiveness. It is up to the community colleges to take action on basic skills development.

HISTORICAL ROOTS

Remedial education is not new. Some critics assume that developmental education began in the 1960s and 1970s when landmark equal opportunity legislation passed. To the contrary, developmental education's historical roots can be traced to Harvard University (nee College) as far back as 1636. Since Latin was the language of learning, those students who did not know Latin were immediately given a tutor upon enrollment. The practice of using tutors remained common until after the American Revolution and the gradual transition to texts and instruction written in English (Boylan and White 1987).

Although American higher education dates back to the founding of Harvard College, the concept of developing an educated citizenry was born in 1837 with the establishment of the Massachusetts common schools. The formation of these schools marked the beginning of free education in this country. Before this period, higher education had been a privilege reserved for the young adult children of wealthy aristocrats.

Access to higher education expanded during the Jacksonian Democracy period, but since most colleges and universities of this period had to be self-sustaining, their recruitment efforts targeted wealthy prospects whether or not they were academically prepared to begin college-level work. They were "automatically 'college material'" (Boylan and White 1987, 2) if they had the funds to enroll. To alleviate the problem of underprepared students, colleges and universities hired even more tutors—so many, in fact, that "many colleges had more people involved in giving and receiving tutoring than were involved in delivering and taking classes" (Boylan and White 1987, 2).

During higher education's early years, skill-deficient students were abundant in numbers and eagerly welcomed on campuses, but a shift in attitude toward underprepared students occurred during the 1800s on many prestigious university campuses, including Yale and Vassar. Unacceptable academic preparation among enrolling freshman students was no longer acceptable. In 1869, Cornell University's president, Andrew D. White, complained that students' "utter ignorance" in the "common English branches" was "astounding"; in 1872, the *Vassar Miscellany* referred to such students as "inferior forms," and, in 1882, as "a vandal horde" (Brier 1984). In 1871, Harvard University president Charles Eliot observed that Harvard freshmen did not know the rudimentary rules of grammar, punctuation, and spelling. He therefore called for the establishment of an entrance examination; half of Harvard's applicants failed that exam but many were admitted "on condition" (Weidner 1990, 4). The Committees on Doubtful Cases reviewed qualifications of underprepared students. In 1882, "[u]nhappy instructors were confronted with immature thoughts set down in a crabbed and slovenly hand, miserably expressed and wretchedly spelled" (4–5).

Colleges and universities thus found themselves taking steps to maintain high academic standards while simultaneously needing to recruit students wealthy enough to afford a college education. To solve this dilemma, many institutions established preparatory departments, widely viewed as institutional embarrassments. Some universities formed committees and held meetings—referred to as "academic 'witch hunts'" (Pintozzi 1987)—to determine the academic preparedness of potential students. Institutions tried valiantly for several years to rid themselves of preparatory programs, but to no avail—the need was too great, and it finally outweighed the embarrassment.

As our nation expanded westward, so did the need for access to higher education. Businesses and agriculture alike put pressure on institutions to develop higher skilled workers. To meet these demands, the Act of 1862 Donating Lands for Colleges of Agriculture and Mechanic Arts (the First Morrill Act) and the Act of 1890 Providing for the Further Endowment and Support of Colleges of Agriculture and Mechanic Arts (the Second Morrill Act) were passed. The First Morrill Act established land-grant institutions, thereby opening the doors for America's industrial and agricultural classes to attend college. As a result, America began witnessing the death of the traditional concept that higher education was a reserved right and privilege of society's elite. "These colleges gave credence to the concept of the 'people's college,' a term [now] widely used to describe community colleges" (Vaughan 1982, 11).

The Second Morrill Act stimulated the growth of black colleges and universities, by allowing black people access to higher education—including those who previously had been denied a basic education by southern law. The majority of students entering these institutions took classes to learn and develop basic skills. The tremendous contributions of these historically black colleges and universities to access and to developmental education have been largely ignored, and yet "their entire mission might be defined as remedial and developmental" (Boylan and White 1987, 4). Their philosophy echoes that of developmental education: "[I]f we do not [develop our students] . . . then who will?" (Jones and Richards-Smith 1987, 2).

Access to higher education expanded in 1901–02 with the creation of the first junior college. There was some disagreement, even among its supporters, as to why a junior college should be created. The idea originated with University of Chicago president William Rainey Harper, who proposed that junior colleges be established to provide skill-deficient students an additional two-year time period to prepare for senior college work. To some, junior colleges gave high school graduates two more years to consider potential careers. To others, the purpose was training individuals—primarily men—who intended to transfer to four-year institutions in pursuit of a baccalaureate degree (Vaughan 1982). Still others viewed this newly established institution as vocational—providing technical training to mechanically minded men and home economics training to domestically minded women (Eells 1931). A few believed junior colleges separated unprepared or otherwise unqualified students from university settings (Brubacher and Rudy 1958). Similarly, others insisted that junior colleges took lesser students so the higher education institutions could do the job for which they were intended—preparing the professional elite for their careers (Zwerling 1976; Roueche and Roueche 1993).

Although the open-door concept was well established by the 1940s, the Servicemen's Readjustment Act of 1944 (the GI Bill of Rights) allowed returning World War II veterans greater access to junior colleges. This bill, whose benefits extended to subsequent veterans of military campaigns as well, provided education scholarships for more than seven million veterans. The GI Bill, in fact, was the legislative act that enabled the formation of a large middle class in America. Moreover, this legislation marked the beginning of the federal government's commitment that monetary need should not deny anyone the opportunity to enroll in college.

Before the GI Bill, faculty and higher education leaders maintained that limiting enrollment was essential to maintaining traditionally high standards. Faculty and administrators discovered the value of a diverse student population when the veterans arrived on campus. Colleges profited from their new students; they were more mature, experienced, and eager to learn. Although motivated, many veterans performed poorly on assessment tests. If these students were to be academically successful, colleges needed to provide even more student services.

In 1947, the Truman Commission on Higher Education first promulgated the concept of education for everyone. Recognizing the new role of the United States as a global advocate for democracy, the commission viewed universal access to higher education as essential to promote national democratic ideals. To illustrate how revolutionary the commission's thinking was, consider these facts. The commission deemed that 49 percent of the population had the ability to complete advanced degrees. Yet only six percent of the entire white population held four-year college degrees (Vaughan and Associates 1983). Even high school graduation rates for white males and females were only 18 and 23 percent, respectively.

To accommodate the increased enrollment, the Truman Commission advocated expanding the two-year college system. The subsequent legislation established the primary functions of community colleges and served as a federal incentive for states and communities to participate in the growing community college network. The increased availability of student aid expanded access. Legislation, beginning with the Higher Education Act of 1965 and followed by subsequent amendments and reauthorizations in 1972 and 1992, increased available opportunities in higher education for all Americans. One critical element of this legislation, the Pell Grant, is still a financial-aid option for undergraduates. Colleges again experienced a tremendous enrollment increase, including poor, disadvantaged, and minority students—many of whom came from "the lower quartile of their [high school] graduating class and from the lower socioeconomic segment of society" (Vaughan and Associates 1983, 25). Higher education, especially the community colleges, witnessed a steady increase in the number of underprepared students, thus warranting additional increases in remedial services.

Critics emerged during this period citing community colleges' "revolving doors" and "cooling out" practices (Roueche and Roueche 1993). Remediation in higher education had escaped the intrusive and mandatory policies for change that have been occurring in other educational arenas. But that is changing, as remedial education in higher education is dismantled by politicians responding to their own and their constituents' concerns and demands.

BALANCING ACCESS AND EXCELLENCE

Historically, community colleges had differing missions and goals, depending on the local community needs. But their founding principles were similar. They believed that higher education was the right of any person who could profit from it and that colleges existed to serve the people. The American education system, of which community colleges are a part, embodies the ideas that education is essential to maintaining a democracy and improving society, and that education is key to equalizing opportunity for all citizens. While time has produced many changes in higher education, this philosophy continues intact and serves as a foundation for today's community colleges.

WHERE ARE WE NOW?

Today, community colleges find themselves in the difficult position of defending the open-access concept. The foremost question is: Can community colleges continue to provide quality educational programs while providing open-access opportunities to those same programs? In response,

K. Patricia Cross and other researchers observe that the open-access model, by itself, will not fulfill the promise of equal opportunity without improved instruction and changes to the curriculum.

Many critics, quick to blame the open-access concept for the decline of academic standards, insist that the push in the 1960s for equality and opportunity compromised the commitment to excellence and high academic standards. Critics further contend that universal open access has the appearance of being an egalitarian practice, but in reality it gives many students the false impression that they do not have to work hard in high school because they will have another chance later on. Supporters insist open access was essential to provide college admission to anyone having a desire to learn. Somewhere along the line, higher education lost sight of the purpose behind open access, which was not merely to permit students to enter colleges, but to enable them to learn.

Today, open access is threatened as a direct result of demands for accountability and increased focus on developmental education. Some proponents of open access fear that the growing demands for accountability and quality might limit—or worse still—close the doors of opportunity to many students. As Cohen suggests, for most community college students "the choice is not between the community college and the senior residential institution; it is between the local college and nothing" (1990, 439).

To maintain open access, community colleges must emphasize the importance of academic achievement and high expectations by all students. As Miami-Dade Community College president emeritus Robert H. McCabe insists: "The goal is excellence for everyone. . . . Ultimately, no one benefits when individuals simply pass through the program and become certified while lacking the competencies indicated by those certifications" (1982–83, 8). To ensure student success, many community colleges have gone to great lengths to meet the diverse needs of their at-risk students. Through hard work, determination, and dedication to student success, these institutions have proven that it is possible to provide open access while maintaining high academic standards; in short, they are living the community college philosophy.

LEGISLATIVE ATTACKS

Developmental education plays a critical role in ensuring student success and lowering student attrition rates. Unfortunately, the positive ramifications of developmental education is often overshadowed by negative attacks focusing on increasing costs, duplication of services, and increasing numbers of skill-deficient students. Much of this criticism stems from policymakers. They are frustrated by the idea that taxpayers are paying twice for educating the same students. However, this idea is not totally accurate. Only half of all high-school graduates go on to college; of these first-time freshmen, approximately 25 percent require some college preparatory work prior to enrolling in regular academic courses. As many as half of the entering freshman class at any community college have not recently been educated at the taxpayers' expense. They are recent immigrants, GED recipients, high school (or earlier years) dropouts, or returning after many years out of the classroom and needing instruction in basic skills.

Policymakers are frustrated, as well, with institutions of higher education themselves—including community colleges. They argue that community colleges and four-year colleges and universities "should increasingly assume that more advanced learning occurs during high school than has in the past—and educate accordingly" (Reising 1997, 172) and that "higher education [must] share blame for the pervasive decline of standards and accountability. . . . Continuing the system of free passes does no one any favor, it only debases . . . American public education" (Moloney 1996, 11A).

In response to these perceived failings of higher education, members of Congress have drafted bills to, among other things, place restrictions on the availability of Title IV funds for the use of developmental course work (Roueche and Roueche 1999). In essence, concerned about increases in federal appropriations, these policymakers propose that grant funds be reallocated to assist better-prepared students. Concerned about equal access, critics insist that such a policy would target and penalize socially and economically disadvantaged students. Expressing similar frustrations with increasing student underpreparedness, many state legislators are taking steps to reform developmental education. Arkansas, Louisiana, Oklahoma, Tennessee, and Virginia have taken legal steps to limit remediation in four-year institutions. In some states, such as Montana, Virginia, and West Virginia, elected officials are reviewing reimbursement proposals. Such measures would serve as both a warranty documenting student skills at graduation, and also as a means of charging local school districts for remediation expenses incurred by the state on behalf of their graduates.

Some higher education systems are revoking their open access policies. In 1997, the Georgia State Board of Regents, choosing a different strategy, imposed more selective admission standards and also voted to reduce and eventually eliminate the percentage of students taking remedial courses by 2001. In a similar fashion, the Massachusetts Board of Higher Education elected to increase its admission criteria and establish limits on the number of freshmen requiring remedial attention on four-year campuses (Blanchette 1997).

Taking a more drastic approach, a South Carolina statute has been enacted to prohibit remedial education in their four-year universities and colleges; the responsibility for developmental education would be relegated to the community colleges. The Florida state legislature not only eliminated remediation from their four-year institutions (except for Florida A&M University) but also placed limitations on the time and funding extended toward remedial course work. For example, the bill stipulates that college students are limited to two attempts to pass each basic skills course. Furthermore, on the second attempt, the student must pay the full cost of instruction or "four times greater than the regular tuition rate" (Ignash 1997, 6).

On the municipal level, New York mayor Rudolph Giuliani publicly chastised the public education system for producing underprepared students. Giuliani advocated eliminating remediation from the community college curriculum and privatizing remedial education. In May 1999, the City University of New York Board of Trustees voted 9 to 6 to approve a plan that altered the system's historic commitment to open admissions and access. Beginning in September 1999, remedial education in most of the system's 11 four-year colleges would be phased out and transferred into the hands of the system's community colleges. Ultimately, this reform has the potential of affecting more than 12,000 new baccalaureate-degree students each year, the majority of whom are people of color (Healy 1998).

Following the examples established by external constituents mandating remedial education, many higher education institutions are beginning to impose remediation restrictions, such as establishing time limits on students taking developmental course work. The National Center for Education Statistics reports that 94 percent of public and 98 percent of private four-year institutions and 41 percent of community colleges responding to its surveys in the mid-1990s have implemented remediation time-limit policies (NCES 1996).

Given recent attacks on remediation, some community college leaders prefer to avoid the topic or to invent excuses for offering developmental course work. On the positive side, Giuliani and others may be doing community colleges a favor: Remedial education needs to be in the national spotlight and receive the attention that it demands if we, as a nation, are to proactively reduce the numbers of basic skill-deficient individuals.

WHERE DO WE GO FROM HERE?

As an educational flash point, remedial education is not going to go away any time soon, nor will skill-deficient students. We believe that remedial and developmental education have important roles to play. Community colleges have been struggling with defining these roles for some time. Some community college leaders have reaffirmed their commitment to universal access. Their institutions tackle the challenges of serving the increasing numbers of skill-deficient students—high-risk behavior, many would warn, in an era of increasing public demands for proof that colleges are effective and deserving of support. Many of these institutions are proving that it is not only possible to provide quality educational programs while providing open-access opportunities, but that student success rates can be improved dramatically overall at the same time.

Our 1999 study *High Stakes, High Performance: Making Remedial Education Work* (Roueche and Roueche) showcased a number of successful strategies for improving remedial education programs—ultimately documented by increased student success rates—being implemented at colleges across the country. However, not a single college had all the pieces in place for an exemplary remedial or developmental program. Moreover, no college had strong, viable data to support claims that its remedial and developmental program strategies had positively affected the entire institution.

Now such a college has emerged. For several years, we had been following one community college's commitment to "valuing diversity"— so serious a commitment that the college had been setting goals, achieving them, and raising the standard on performance every year for more than a decade. The Community College of Denver was committed—faculty, staff, and administrators, heart and soul—to increasing student diversity and student success. We tell the CCD story here because it is extraordinary, because it should be told, and because it offers enormous hope for all colleges—and especially for those who are struggling to win the war against academic underpreparedness, in spite of the odds against them.

The story of the Community College of Denver began more than a decade ago with a decision to change what it was to what it could become, with a commitment to valuing diversity and, ultimately, with a vision of achieving a goal—that every student can be successful. The college does not consider its results extraordinary, but we do. This institution is the perfect response to critics of the open-door college and of efforts to live up to its promises.

2 A Matter of Choice, A Commitment to Act

As the "people's college," the community college has a bright and promising future, but a refusal to serve all persons in the community will mark its decline and eventual demise. This report offers encouragement and proof that the two-year college can "put it all together." Democracy's college may yet be a reality!

—Roueche and Kirk 1973

AN EQUAL OPPORTUNITY COLLEGE

As the leading point of entry to higher education for metropolitan Denver, the Community College of Denver has become one of the premier learning colleges over the past decade. President Byron McClenney refers to CCD as an "equal opportunity college." The college is celebrated for creating a learning environment conducive to the success of all students, valuing diversity, promoting the use of technology by students and faculty, implementing institutional effectiveness, instituting accountability practices—especially in the area of developmental education—and working in its service community to promote and support economic and community development.

In our book *The Company We Keep: Collaboration in the Community College* (Roueche, Taber, and Roueche 1995), CCD president McClenney described the community-wide problems that led to CCD's decision to become a convener and facilitator, smoothing the way for collaborative activities between and among service, business, and educational entities in a city desperately in need of help from a unified effort providing problem-solving strategies.

We had read numerous internal and external reports of CCD's diverse accomplishments, and we were captivated by the array of its community initiatives in the Denver metropolitan area. With our co-author, Lynn Taber, we selected the college—along with 14 others—to contribute to the book, a report studying North American community colleges' partnerships and collaboratives. Each contributor described the catalysts for college decisions to partner and collaborate, the process to select partners, and the most significant experiences. The Community College of Denver's success has spawned a cottage industry of success.

The drumbeat of success has continued for the Community College of Denver. In 1996, Henry Cisneros, then Secretary of Housing and Urban Development, documented CCD's record of successful business partnerships and collaboration efforts in *Hallmarks of Best Practices in Urban Community Colleges*. In 1997, we featured CCD again, along with six other U.S. community colleges, in a broader study of institutional effectiveness. The report, *Embracing the Tiger: The Effectiveness Debate and the Community College* (Roueche, Johnson, and Roueche), showcased colleges successful at collecting appropriate outcome data and then using these data to measure how effective they were in fulfilling the promises made in their mission statements—that is, to assess how well they were achieving specific goals and objectives. Simultaneously, Oblinger and Rush, in *The Learning Revolution* (1997), and O'Banion, in *A Learning College for the 21st Century* (1997), featured CCD as an institution modeling learning college practices.

Still more accolades followed. In 1998, *Managing Change: A Model for Community College Leaders* (Baker) featured CCD and 10 other community colleges as successes in implementing change strategies to realize their core values. In *Developmental Education: A Twenty-First Century Social and Economic Imperative* (McCabe and Day 1998), CCD's developmental education program was identified as a successful model for improving student success. In 1999, O'Banion's *Launching a Learning-Centered College* included CCD as one of four models of a successful learning college environment.

The Public Broadcasting System's adult education series *Author, Author* has twice featured segments on the Community College of Denver. CCD has received numerous national awards and appears frequently in professional journal articles and newspapers. CCD's success has prompted the school to undertake innovative dissemination strategies. Publicity about

CCD's success with at-risk students increased the frequency and number of college visitors, particularly to the developmental education division. Staff and faculty became concerned about the time required by the visits. The college therefore decided to host a national conference in 1999 to share information about CCD's developmental programs, classes, and services. Conference coordinators and steering committee members agreed that an interactive environment, where ideas, concerns, and best practices could be exchanged by presenters and participants, would be their best approach. The college invited other colleges to participate in roundtable discussions. The conference was a success, and plans are under way for a second.

In March 2000, CCD was awarded the Hesburgh Award. Named for Theodore M. Hesburgh, president emeritus of the University of Notre Dame and nationally renowned educator and world-renowned humanitarian, and sponsored by the Teacher's Insurance and Annuity Association and the College Retirement Equities Fund (TIAA-CREF, the national education retirement account), this award recognizes the best professional development program in higher education. Sixty-two colleges and universities across the United States competed for the award. At the 82nd annual meeting of the American Council on Education in Chicago, Illinois, CCD received this honor—and its accompanying check for $30,000—in recognition for its Teaching/Learning Center (T/LC).

The Teaching/Learning Center originated over a decade ago. In 1990, CCD developed a long-range goal of eliminating differences in outcomes for its students of color, following an analysis of 1989 student data that indicated lower retention and graduation rates for students of color than for white students. CCD's T/LC was an outgrowth of that long-range plan. T/LC helps the college produce measurable increases in the recruitment, retention, and graduation rates of students of color by improving and enhancing faculty teaching skills to serve CCD's diverse student body. Enrollments by people of color went from 35 percent of the student body in 1989 to more than 55 percent in 1999—increases CCD links directly to the T/LC program.

Denver's Community

A comparison of census data from 1990 with 1980 shows Denver to be a city in need of positive change. The data reveal these facts:

- Denver's population decreased 5 percent between 1980 and 1990.
- Denver's percentage of Colorado's population fell from 17 percent to 14.2 percent.
- People of color in Denver rose from 33 percent to 39 percent.
- Families with children tended to either move out of Denver or to send their children to private schools.
- Sixty-six percent of public school students are now people of color.
- Middle-income people of color are moving to the suburbs.
- Denver family households headed by a female increased from 26 percent to 31 percent.
- One-third of all Colorado welfare recipients reside in Denver (McClenney 1995, 83–84).

The numbers of at-risk children and young adults increased, the population has lower levels of education and lower salaries, and there are more individuals working in blue-collar and service jobs than a decade ago. Added to those problems are the high incidence of dropouts from all levels of the public schools, especially among students of color (at least 50 percent); the increase in drug and gang activity; and the general economic turndown in Denver, as in many urban areas across the country during that same period.

Institutional Profile

Established as a separate campus in 1976, the Community College of Denver is the third largest of 13 community colleges in the Colorado Community Colleges (CCC, formerly Colorado Community College and Occupational Education System). It is located in the Auraria Higher Education Center Campus in Denver's historical district, sharing some classrooms, laboratories, recreational facilities, a regional library, and a state-of-the-art centrally located student union facility with the Metropolitan State College of Denver (MSCD) and the University of Colorado at Denver.

To better serve the needs of the surrounding communities, CCD established four satellite technical education centers (TEC). Referred to as CCD West, CCD East, CCD North, and Lowry, these centers are situated in Denver's most underprivileged neighborhoods. The centers provide local residents with opportunities to obtain technical and vocational certificates; they also encourage students to complete associate degrees. Moreover, the college runs nine GED institutes in metropolitan Denver to enable potential students to complete basic studies and may encourage them to continue with higher education. The institutes are located at Cheltenham Elementary School, Denver Employment First, Cross Community Coalition, The Gathering Place, the Life Development Institute, the Native American Multicultural Center, North Lincoln, The Spot, and on the CCD campus. Additional centers are located in Adams County at Career Enrichment Park, Thornton United Presbyterian Church, Access Housing, and CCD North.

Drawing from more than 160 public and private Colorado schools, CCD is a major higher education entry point for urban high school graduates. That was not the case in fall 1986, when only six graduates from Denver high schools enrolled at CCD; by 1993–94, more than 600 local students matriculated at CCD. This number continues to rise annually.

CCD currently serves more than 10,000 students—twice that of 15 years ago. More than 30 percent of these students are 20 years of age or younger, approximately 55 percent are persons of color, and 60 percent are the first generation of their families to attend college (McClenney and Flores 1998). CCD is typical of other large urban community colleges in that the majority of its students come from the poor neighborhoods of the inner city. Primarily, the student population is Latino, American Indian, African American, and Asian American—all struggling financially to enroll and stay in college.

For almost all CCD students, finances pose a major obstacle in achieving educational success. CCD staff members work to link students and external agencies, to provide essential financial aid information and potential options for work-study employment, and to identify policies of entities that could act at cross-purposes to restrict or to deny students viable options for financing their college work. Because the average family income represented among CCD students is slightly more than $10,000 annually, Pell grants are a major potential source of financial aid (Table 2.1). As a proactive measure, in addition to tabulating Pell grant recipients annually (e.g., 2,025 in 1996 at CCD), CCD also tracks the nonrecipients who are struggling financially, for they are even more at-risk of dropping out of college when time and energy constraints become unmanageable.

Table 2.1 Pell Grant Distribution among Colorado Community Colleges

College	Fall 1997 Minority Enrollments	Average (Pell) Family Income	1996 Pell Grant Recipients
Pueblo Community College	1,546 (33.5%)	$12,339	1,736
Trinidad State Junior College	1,102 (43.8%)	$13,278	924
Community College of Denver	3,274 (54.5%)	$10,395	2,025
State Average	24%	$14,275	

An even more unfortunate situation for CCD students is tuition costs. Significantly higher than the national community college average, CCD's tuition is another major financial barrier to higher education. Only four cities nationwide—New York City, Boston, Philadelphia, and Baltimore— report college tuition and fees higher than those of CCD (Table 2.2). CCD works to overcome that barrier through innovative ways to lighten students' financial burdens (see Chapter 3).

Table 2.2 Community College Tuition and Fees Compared by Major National City

City	Tuition and Fees (30 Semester Hours)
New York City	$2,600
Denver	$1,884
Seattle	$1,502
Chicago	$1,400
Atlanta	$1,266
Phoenix	$1,120
San Diego	$412

Source: B. McClenney, personal communication, February 1999.

CCD is the only higher education institution in Colorado that does not have an ethnic or racial majority (McClenney and Flores 1998). The college embodies its philosophy that all students are entitled equally to a quality education, that education "must provide the student with an understanding and appreciation of our interdependence as individuals and a nation . . . must be meaningful to multi-ethnic students," and must "provide the student body, faculty, and staff with an understanding of cultural pluralism" (*CCD Facts 1998–99,* 9). To achieve this educational environment, CCD has dedicated more than a decade to fostering "cultural diversity, international understanding, and global awareness" (*CCD Facts 1998–99*, 9). The college claims it has earned the label by which it describes itself—an equal opportunity college. Three other benchmarks help CCD gauge better the success of minority students:

- In 1991, for the first time, people of color had higher transfer rates than did white students.
- In 1998, for the first time, cohort tracking indicated no significant difference in student success on the basis of race, ethnicity, age, or gender.
- In 1999, for the first time, the percentage of minorities among graduates and transfers topped 50 percent.

The significance of these statistics is heightened when the array of difficulties facing students of color—especially returning women—are considered. Many women report they face cultural barriers that make continuing their education critically problematic; many confess they live with a disapproving family. Such serious disapproval often outweighs the student's desire to continue her education, and she drops out of college.

Students of color may bring the challenges of cultural diversity to a college, but almost all students bring the challenges of academic diversity to the classroom. Developmental education is a major enterprise at CCD; this college delivers one-third of all remedial instruction statewide—especially remarkable when one considers that the Colorado higher education system comprises 28 colleges and universities. Developmental education accounts for one third of the college's total credit hours (McClenney and Flores 1998).

Although the developmental student profile mirrors that of CCD's general student population, there are some unique characteristics. Students enrolled in developmental courses represent an older student cohort—ranging in age from the mid- to late twenties and well into the seventies. The average age in the total student population remains at 28 years, with nearly one third age 20 years or younger.

The developmental population includes high school dropouts, under-prepared high school graduates with learning disabilities and social deficiencies, adults returning to college for retraining, mothers receiving welfare, and immigrants requiring English as a second language (ESL) assistance.

Researchers have yet to reach a common definition or description of the "typical" developmental student. A sizable list of student characteristics has been developed from studies, and many of them may be applied to the majority of students needing remedial or developmental work prior to enrolling in college-level work. Although underpreparedness appears in all ethnic, racial, and socioeconomic classes, at-risk students are disproportionately minority and poor, poverty is their most common denominator. This is true of CCD's developmental student population. While no common definition has been offered, most researchers agree that a combination of demographic and societal changes are creating the remedial student of today.

In recent years, the hard work and dedication to a quality developmental program have paid off with these "firsts":

- 1995 was the first year that students who began in developmental education were as likely to graduate as students not requiring assistance when they enrolled.
- 1998 was the first year that developmental education completion became a predictor of success (after graduation and/or transfer).

Currently, more than 48 percent of the Denver Public School system's total student population is Latino. Denver Public School attrition rates, using a four-year tracking system that begins in the ninth grade, revealed that fewer than half of the Latino students graduated from high school. CCD has determined that this accounts for large numbers of Hispanic students in their developmental education courses. With the overall dropout rate in Denver now nearing 50 percent for all ethnic groups, CCD administrators and developmental education personnel fear that the Latino numbers are a harbinger of things to come.

Based on current high school dropout rates and using truancy at age 16 as a predictor, students are leaving public schools at younger ages every year. Children of migrant workers are leaving school as early as the third grade to help with family responsibilities.

Although the circumstances that contribute to students' need for developmental education differ—for example, a mother on welfare with several children sees this chance as hope for a better life, or a youth offender needs a way to combat life on the streets—they share common elements. Most remedial students fear failing, believe they are not smart enough to succeed at college-level work, fear being "found out" by an academic system and forced out, and are apprehensive and angry toward an education system that, for all practical purposes, has discarded them. CCD talks openly about combating these feelings. The college seeks to bring these students up to speed quickly, providing an orientation to the culture of this college and the larger higher education world, and providing valuable time for career planning, goal setting, problem solving, and communication skills development.

As a result of Denver's large immigrant population, the demand continues to escalate for ESL courses. Within CCD's developmental education division, ESL is a close second in full-time employees to the reading department. Although ESL enrollment figures fluctuate, the typical semester headcount is between 400 and 700 students. While battling a language barrier in this country, most ESL students report a strong academic history in their native countries; they merely lack the English language skills required to complete college-level courses in the United States.

The college is responding to the effects of today's changing technologies on the city's current workforce and the potential workforce of its future. Between plant closures, downsizing strategies, and business takeovers, CCD frequently finds itself serving individuals who find themselves unemployed after 15 or 20 years of service. In these cases, the college handles not only retraining issues, but also the trickle-down effects of unemployment—the fear of losing families, homes, and self-esteem. The age diversity of CCD's student population creates a special challenge for a college committed to success for all students.

COLORADO'S DEMANDS FOR INSTITUTIONAL EFFECTIVENESS

In 1996, the Colorado General Assembly initiated House Bill 96-1219— the Higher Education Quality Assurance Act. Specifically, the new law mandated that the state define in clear terms its expectations for higher education and insisted on the development of a quality indicator system for measuring whether and the degree to which higher education is meeting the state's goals and expectations. This new legislation followed previous initiatives requiring the establishment of a postsecondary performance indicator system. Both legislative mandates were a result of external constituent pressure demanding increased accountability from public higher education institutions.

Recognizing the need to respond to these demands, the Colorado Commission on Higher Education contracted the National Center for Higher Education Management Systems (NCHEMS) to develop a set of clear and objective performance indicators meeting Colorado legislative specifications. "NCHEMS brought a valuable comparative perspective to the task, since the organization was conducting similar exercises in a variety of states" (Smith 1998, 3). NCHEMS conducted statewide focus groups to collect input to draft an initial set of performance indicators focused mainly on outcomes. The commissioners reviewed the indicators and asked staff to work directly with the Colorado institutional research community to "further refine and develop the indicators" (3) and reduce the number of indicators.

In response, commission staff and institutional researchers from across the state began to revise the indicators. This group, known as the Technical Committee, focused on the ability to collect, analyze, and present the data. At the same time, a second independent group, known as the Policy Group, met regularly with commission staff to ensure that the indicator system was meeting the specifications set forth by their individual governing boards and institutions. After months of intense work, the commission voted in April 1997 to approve nine statewide quality indicators "with the proviso that it was acting in a phased approach toward final approval of the entire set of indicators required under HB 96-1219" (3).

Under a proviso established by HB 96-1219, the State Board for Community Colleges and Occupational Education (SBCCOE) elected to develop an additional six indicators for measuring institutional effectiveness at the community college level. By adopting the additional indicators, the SBCCOE wanted to ensure that the system quality indicators were unique to community colleges and would "generate the requisite data to measure each community college's achievement of statewide goals and expectations for higher education" (Smith 1998, 2). In June 1997, these six indicators, along with indicators developed by other higher education institutions and governing boards, received final approval by the Colorado Commission on Higher Education.

THE REPORT CARD

Currently, the majority of CCD's institutional effectiveness monitoring is driven by these common quality indicators:

- After-graduation performance
- Undergraduate student success rates
- Student satisfaction
- Advising
- Employer satisfaction
- Technology plan
- Assessment and accountability
- K–12 linkages and teacher preparation
- Business partnerships
- Faculty and staff development
- Access to education
- Enhancing campus diversity
- Student satisfaction with services
- Responsiveness to service area needs

After one year, CCD had met or exceeded statewide averages in all areas of reporting. Over the past 10 years, CCD has focused its efforts on student achievement, institutional effectiveness, and accountability, striving to make additional progress in each area each year. The 1997–98 results illustrate some of CCD's most noteworthy successes.

Table 2.3 Community College of Denver versus the Average: Performance Indicators, 1997–98

Indicators	Community Colleges Overall	Commission Targets	CCD Results
Graduates' satisfaction	86.1%	90%	95.1%
Instructional satisfaction	93.7%	90%	98.8%
Administrative services satisfaction	83.3%	90%	
Student services satisfaction	83.6%	90%	93%
Nontraditional classes	28%		55%
Minority student reenrollment	25.3%		

A COMMITMENT TO DOING THE RIGHT THINGS RIGHT

We have alluded to 1986 as a pivotal year in the Community College of Denver's existence. But what precisely occurred? The process began at the spring 1986 convocation, when CCD faculty and staff were asked to participate as a group to identify possible goals for the future development of their institution. Although skeptical and surprised, the group came together to prioritize goal statements that had been provided for their consideration. The results were published in the college newspaper. The consensus institutional vision focused on developing "an institution where students would come first and where collaboration would be the manner in which work would be done" (McClenney 1997a, 71).

The next step was to ask the planning council to perform an environmental scan (McClenney 1997a, 72), which entailed tracking the pattern of student movement throughout the institution. All faculty and staff received the results as a series of background papers for the 1987 spring convocation.

At the convocation, the faculty and staff divided into smaller discussion groups to develop strategies in response to the results of the environmental scan. The discussion yielded a set of priorities for the following year. This process, viewed as a success, has become an annual institutional exercise to evaluate the results of one year and set the strategies for the next. In addition, the college bases funding allocation on these priorities. In this manner, faculty and staff brainstorm annually as a team about CCD's future directions.

THE PLANNING PROCESS

CCD has an effective method of evaluating goals and achievements, institutional vision, and annual action priorities. To ensure the validity of the process, a concise planning model is followed each year.

In the initial stages, institutional effectiveness data are collected in the following areas:

- General education skills/knowledge
- Discipline-specific skills/knowledge
- Retention and completion
- Student, graduate, alumni, and employer satisfaction; and
- Postgraduate performance

Additional information includes the following:

- Academic profile
- Follow-up surveys
- Satisfaction surveys
- Perkins requirements
- Legislative and CCHE mandates. (This information is consolidated into an annual accountability report.)

The data are forwarded to the planning council—composed of 11 to 13 members from the Auraria campus and the technical education centers.

The annual planning council is a standing committee that finalizes the priorities each year after reviewing the data and the input from the spring brainstorming session and monitors progress toward the goals throughout the year. The council is also used to make ad hoc adjustments and to receive critical input between annual evaluations. While most council members leave after serving one year, some may be invited by the president to serve another year to provide continuity in discussions and planning, or to maintain diverse representation of the college community. Individuals may be nominated or may volunteer to join. Current council members do not nominate only individuals who will represent their particular areas; rather, there is a concerted effort to have a broad representation of all college groups and levels. However, representatives of instruction and student services are always on the council. The names of all individuals, nominees, and volunteers are submitted to the president; all are accepted for membership and invited to serve. When deemed necessary, the president will add members to achieve adequate diversity and guarantee equal representation. This democratic process is an accepted and respected process.

The planning council solicits input from faculty and staff, standing committees, councils, centers, and the main campus. The council uses the input as it reviews the mission statement and develops the goals and objectives and five action priorities. After these tasks have been accomplished, the documents describing the data collected and the strategies for achieving the action priorities are prepared and distributed to units (e.g., arts and humanities or financial aid) to use in developing unit plans. Next, the unit plans are consolidated into a college plan for the year. The entire college sets common goals, although strategies among the college units may differ. This grassroots format promotes universal buy-in from all levels of college activities and services.

> *The resulting plan always includes the achievements and results for the current year; desirable outcomes for next year; projections for the second year and beyond; and priorities for personnel, equipment, and projects. Unit plans are combined into area plans for instruction, student services, administrative services, campus centers (Technical Education Centers), and the president's staff. (McClenney 1997a, 74–75)*

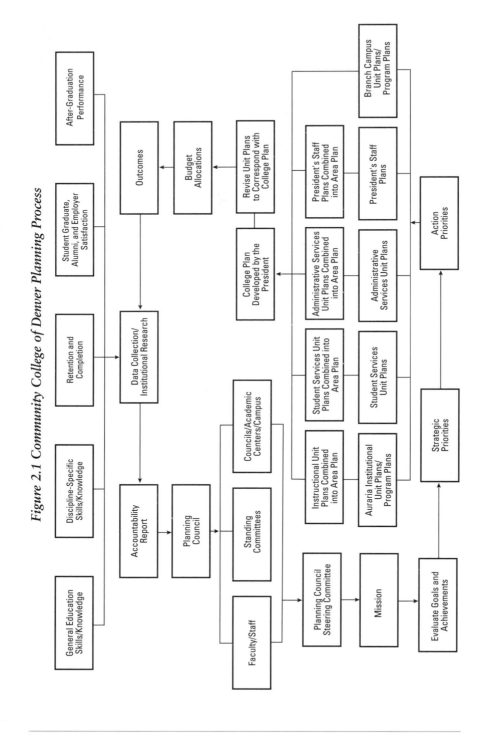

Figure 2.1 Community College of Denver Planning Process

A two-page limit is set for all plans, regardless of level or area, in order to help participants focus on the most critical information. In addition, all unit and area plans must be submitted within the two-week period provided for that activity.

The president is responsible for the final review and consolidation of the ideas into a coherent plan. The president may require unit plans to be revised to ensure that they correspond with the college plan. "Line-item budgeting does not begin until the plan has been circulated and leaders have had a chance to make adjustments to their respective plans" (McClenney 1997a, 75). The president, the vice president of administrative services, and the vice president of information resources and planning use the final product to allocate the budget. The final step is to execute the college plan and the individual area plans. Periodic evaluation—a critical element—guarantees proper implementation of all plans.

The annual planning process not only provides an internal means of examining institutional effectiveness but is tied to external accountability mandates by the Colorado Commission on Higher Education and the North Central Association of Colleges and Schools. During the first year of the process, the focus was on institutional planning and development; the second year's cycle examined the actual means of measuring effectiveness within the institution.

SERVING ITS COMMUNITY

As they conducted the initial environmental scan of their service area during the academic year 1986–87, CCD faculty and staff became disheartened and frightened, then resolved. They felt compelled to take action to improve their own community. Furthermore, the papers they were preparing could help describe action plans for community development. As they researched population characteristics and trends, and the community's economic and social priorities, they amassed critical evidence of a community in need of help. Their reports documented the following:

- Unemployment/underemployment/poverty
- High illiteracy rates
- Economic underdevelopment
- Lack of adequate job training
- Problems in the welfare system

- Insufficient access to education and employment for people of color
- Multiple demands on single heads of households
- High public school dropout rates
- Inadequate levels of available child care
- Limited support for small businesses
- Challenges faced by special populations, such as the disabled or those with limited English proficiency (McClenney 1995, 85)

When CCD's role was debated early on, it was clear the college was but one of many public entities responsible for the community's well-being. What could the college do to help its community rebound economically and grow, and how would its actions be perceived by others who were working on similar goals?

Faculty and administrators realized that agencies with a single or limited focus had not been able to improve the city's plight. Moreover, there was no indication that any community-based agency was in the position to understand all of the issues that needed to be addressed, much less to act effectively. CCD believed the environmental scan had identified the majority of its community's problems. CCD faculty and staff felt confident they had the perspectives, skills, and resources to become a positive force. Ultimately, the college would best serve its community as a facilitator, an entity that convenes critical collaborative efforts by community agencies to solve common problems.

In deciding to assume this role, the college knew it would have to respond to a number of internal and external constituents' concerns—among them, that the college was acting outside the parameters of its mission, attempting to become a social service agency, or establishing itself as a competitor with already established community-based organizations. Initially, the college responded (and ultimately proved) it was neither intending to become a social service agency nor a competitor with other community-based entities; and it went forward to design and implement a role for itself that since has become a critical piece of its success puzzle—collaboration with community.

ACCREDITATION AGENCY APPLAUDS COLLEGE

In 1993, following an extensive review of the college, the North Central Association of Colleges and Schools Accreditation (NCA) team highly recommended granting continued accreditation to the Community College of Denver at the associate degree level. The accreditation process involved analyses of college documents and interviews with all administrators; representatives from all other personnel groups, including staff, faculty, and students; the State Board and College Advisory Council members; and community activists. During in-depth investigation, the team discovered:

> The College [was] well prepared for its on-site evaluation for continued accreditation, but also found a College that had addressed all concerns raised in previous site visits, a College that had used creativity to handle resource issues, and a College that had put in place exemplary planning and accountability activities. (NCA 1993, 45)

The accreditation team noted the creative and determined manner in which the college addressed its ongoing financial difficulties. Although the actual dollars from the state had increased, the percentage of the college budget covered by these dollars had decreased. Since additional funding from the state was unavailable, the college sought new funding through grants from federal, state, and private entities. During the grant-acquiring process, the college formed many long-term partnerships—several of which still exist today. In addition, the college procured additional funding through its entrepreneurial operations and corporate contracts.

In their final report NCA complimented CCD on how it approached the Colorado accountability mandate and the NCA assessment of student academic achievement mandate. In short, CCD had accomplished all of the requests made by the accrediting agencies—to evaluate seriously what the college was doing and then use the documented information to improve its current performance and outcomes.

As detailed earlier, the process used to derive the initial planning initiative was the result of an all-college collaboration to help shape the future of CCD and to determine the funding allocation based on selected priorities. A major step in this process involved determining the accountability indicators for measuring success. The process—involving administrators, faculty, staff, and advisory groups—has become an annual effort. According to the accreditation team, "As a result, the accountability and effectiveness measurements are part of the College fabric, and the results are seen as starting points for next year's efforts. . . . The process is in theory and in practice a complete cycle. . . . This College uses the data to improve retention, to ask itself just what it is looking for in teaching, how can it assist students who enter with lower academic skills, and what assistance do teachers need to do a better job (NCA 1993, 46–47).

During the initial process, diversity was determined to be a major priority. The college, as a group of individuals, was determined "to have the face of the college reflect the face of Denver" (NCA 1993, 47). From employment practices to the art displayed in its halls, CCD instills this philosophy. Persons of color account for 55 percent of the total CCD enrollment of more than 10,000.

REORGANIZATION

More than a decade ago, Ernest Boyer, then president of the Carnegie Foundation for the Advancement of Teaching, addressed the challenges of teaching in a multicultural world before a large audience of community college leaders. He emphasized the critical need to teach students the interconnectedness of the world's various cultures—their common interests and experiences with living and dying, work and leisure, celebrations and concerns; to relate our academic disciplines to real-life experiences; and to pay more teaching and learning attention to ideas and issues, rather than disparate parts of an unorganized whole. He urged educators to look with new eyes on the curriculum of the future by abandoning the isolationism of disciplines in the traditional college curriculum to design future studies around the things we need to know to improve our collective lives, attend to the institutional features that draw individuals into a family of learners, and instill a sense of family to improve teaching and learning at all levels (Boyer 1992).

CCD has taken such steps as coalescing its curriculum, creating a more organized context for learning, and involving all constituents of the college in improving the learning enterprise. These efforts are reflected in CCD's recent program reorganization—primarily of its instructional components—deemed necessary to meet the financial demands established by the college's 1999–2000 action priorities.

The vice president of instruction first solicited suggestions, proposals, and designs, either in person or in writing, from members of the entire campus community. After consolidating the information into three different instructional designs, the entire campus was invited to an open forum to examine, discuss, and arrive at a consensus about a single plan. Participants were reminded that "consensus" meant general agreement, not majority rules. Minor modifications to the chosen plan would be considered if the proponents could make a good argument for change. This democratic, grassroots process gave all faculty and staff affected by the change an opportunity to voice their concerns and opinions, and also gave all participants a sense of ownership and commitment to the project.

The group decided reorganization was to:

- Strengthen program identities through a closer alignment of similar and supporting programs and prefixes
- Provide a stronger identity for students in programs
- Respond to the critical nature of the college's funding and budget allocations by reducing costs

Ultimately, the outcome of the realignment resulted in the configuration of five interconnected centers (formerly called divisions), including:

- Center for Language, Arts, and Behavioral Sciences
- Center for Business and Corporate Development
- Center for Educational Advancement
- Center for Health, Math, and Science
- Center for Learning Outreach

In the reorganization documents, each center was charged with remaining independent of the others by having its own identity, yet was required to recognize instructional connections and shared responsibilities. Each was encouraged to "think outside the box," to expand boundaries, but also to collaborate and communicate with the other centers to achieve the shared college goal of improved student services.

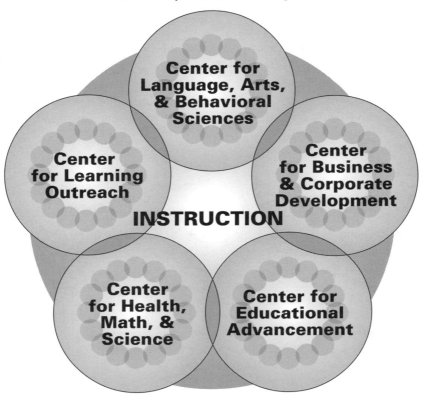

*Figure 2.2 Community College of Denver
21st-Century Instructional Alignment*

With the reorganization, new job descriptions were written for center deans, campus team coordinators, and program/team coordinators. Faculty were given the opportunity to apply for the positions of campus team coordinator (for as much as 6 percent release time) and program/team coordinator (for as much as 4 percent release time) and to accept redefined job responsibilities while they were serving as coordinators. Training for individuals in these positions was conducted during the summer months.

While essential to CCD's financial survival, change was not easy. Despite their involvement, employees feared losing their jobs. The president and vice president of instruction countered this anxiety through written communications and informational meetings.

Figure 2.3 Critical Realignment for Collaborative Thinking

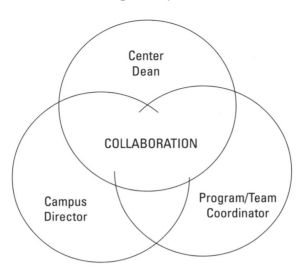

In coordination with the restructuring efforts, the college offered an early retirement option to employees meeting the plan's retirement specifications. The opportunity proved to be an excellent win-win situation for both the college and the retirees, especially since institutional downsizing was inevitable. Although the financial ramifications will be felt in the short term, the long-range cost savings should be significant.

Enrollment is critical to the institution's financial stability. All areas of the college are working together to increase enrollment by improving customer service and marketing. For example, the Instructional Team and Student Services meet regularly to improve customer service in the advising process; results of their efforts include fewer "undeclared" students, a "one-stop-shop," and a more inviting Web site. CCD's instructional realignment is best explained by the user-friendly document "Who Does What and Whom Do I Call?" shown in Table 2.4.

Table 2.4 Who Does What and Whom Do I Call?

Curriculum	
Center Dean	Ultimate responsibility
Campus Director	Is in touch with community needs/keeps informed
Program/Team Coordinator	Coordinates development and revisions regardless of pedagogy/delivery methods; coordinates student advising for all students in or interested in program; involves all full-time faculty and as many part-time instructors as possible
Coordinators' "How-To"	With all faculty, coordinator annually reviews all curriculum and makes needed changes. Dean reviews and approves; coordinator sends changes to catalog coordinator. Follow same process for new courses, new programs; include state approval process for new programs; works with educational case manager to assign students to adviser
Supervision and Evaluation	
Center Dean	All program/team coordinators and full-time faculty in the center and classified staff in center office
Campus Director	Classified staff in campus office and case managers at campus
Program/Team Coordinator	Part-time instructors (some coordinators are piloting supervising full-time faculty)
Coordinators' "How-To"	In collaboration with dean, recruits and recommends for hire all part-time instructors for program; participates in selection process for full-time faculty; ensures all part-time instructors are evaluated by students and that classroom observations are completed in timely manner, regardless of campus or delivery method
Budget Development and Management	
Center Dean	Ultimate responsibility for all budgets associated with the center
Campus Director	Responsible for campus operational budget, capital budget, and part-time instructor dollars for those teaching at the campus
Program/Team Coordinator	Responsible for developing and managing program/prefix operating and capital budgets and part-time instructor dollars associated with the program/prefix

Table 2.4, continued

Coordinators' "How-To"	During annual planning process, follows guidelines and time frame for instruction; develops program budget and presents to dean; if program is represented on more than one campus, confers with campus director(s) re part-time dollars needed for campus; receives and reviews final budget allocation following college allocation from state; requests all part-time instructor contracts and purchase requests; uses procurement card for program expenses; receives and reviews monthly financial reports
Planning	
Center Dean	Overall unit planning
Campus Director	Planning for the campus
Program/Team Coordinator	Annual planning for the program/prefix; creates annual and semester schedule of classes; involves all full-time faculty and as many part-time instructors as possible
Coordinators' "How-To"	Meets with all full-time faculty and as many part-time instructors as possible to develop each semester's schedule of classes; works with campus director(s) to schedule branch campus classes; ensures all classes, regardless of campus or delivery method, are integrated into schedule; involves all faculty and instructors in developing program goals and action plans; monitors progress toward goals during the year
Workload Assignments	
Center Dean	Ultimate responsibility for all faculty and staff; direct assignments for program/team coordinators
Campus Director	Classified staff and case managers assigned to the campus
Program/Team Coordinator	All full-time faculty and part-time instructors teaching within the program/prefix; involves all full-time faculty and as many part-time instructors as possible
Coordinators' "How-To"	Assigns classes and other responsibilities to all part-time instructors; collaboratively develops workload assignments with all full-time faculty teaching in program, including assigning classes and advising responsibilities
Daily Operations	
Center Dean	All center operations
Campus Director	All campus operations, including facilities management and classroom/lab assignments
Program/Team Coordinator	Coordinates classroom/lab assignments with campus directors and dean; ensures supplies are adequate and timely
Coordinators' "How-To"	Orders program supplies; monitors program budget; works with dean and campus director to ensure faculty and instructors receive needed clerical support

Faculty, staff, and students believe this college has a special formula for success. We are convinced these are the key elements to CCD's results:

- Strong administrative leadership
- Positive institutional philosophy, attitude, support, and commitment toward developmental education
- Excellent developmental education faculty
- Centralized developmental education approach
- Quality assessment, advising, and developmental education program formats
- Ongoing diversity efforts

A MATTER OF CHOICE

Kay McClenney, vice president of the Education Commission of the States, and Byron McClenney, CCD president, collaborated on an article on institutional effectiveness for *Community, Technical, and Junior College Journal*. More than a decade has passed since they offered this description of an effective community college:

> *It has a strong sense of purpose and is shaped by the economic and social needs of its service area. It is student-centered, and its effectiveness is measured in terms of both student educational intent and goals achieved. It supports and strengthens the central processes of teaching and learning. Planning, problem solving, and priority setting are shared between administration and faculty, as is the vision of the college role in the community and society. Its leadership is proactive in forging ahead to set new institutional standards. Finally, the effective community college examines itself with a new emphasis on learning outcomes and results as well as processes and resources. (McClenney and McClenney 1988, 58)*

Clearly, distinct parallels can be drawn between this description, the goals that the Community College of Denver has pursued, and the documented success in its solid record of achievements. Arguably, CCD embodies the high standards in this description. They are the standards we hope will describe, ultimately, the goals and achievements of America's most effective community colleges.

If their description was being revised in 2000, another critical characteristic would be added. Kay McClenney articulated that characteristic in an address to the participants at the 1998 National Institute for Staff and Organizational Development (NISOD) International Conference on Teaching and Leadership Excellence:

> *For more than a decade I have been watching the transformational process in one particular community college—at the Community College of Denver. I have watched while, with tight resources, CCD's people have doubled enrollment, while also dramatically increasing student diversity and student outcomes, defining methods of assessing and documenting student learning, and most incredibly, virtually eliminating the achievement gap between minority and non-minority students. It did take ten years of work.* But the first thing it took was deciding to do it. *(K. M. McClenney 1998, 4, emphasis added)*

An organization that decides to change itself, and annually (or according to a scheduled cycle) raises the bar on its own performance, must rely on the combined talents and the individuals who could and will most affect the outcomes of the decision. Most educators are taught various decision-making techniques sometime in their formal training, and all educators experience or revisit these processes on the job. No one would argue that "how" decisions are made can set the stage for good times or bad, ultimate success or failure. We have described what we know about the decision "to do it," and we turn now to CCD's next steps. However, we will revisit the "how" again as a critical leadership issue in the concluding chapter.

Eyes on Success Against the Odds: Putting the Right Pieces Together

> If colleges are totally committed to being successful with at-risk students, they must be prepared to think holistically . . . stand-alone services or classes—no matter how successful in helping at-risk students—will not achieve a college's larger goal of retaining these students and helping them achieve their own goals of improved performance and academic success.
>
> **—Roueche and Roueche 1999**

The Community College of Denver is atypical of most U.S. community colleges. It is the most diverse higher education institution in the state of Colorado, yet it ranks higher than most Colorado community colleges' averages on the statewide Quality Indicators—and higher than all on some. Most of CCD's students are younger than the average community college student, more economically and academically at-risk—CCD provides fully one-third of all remedial instruction in the state—and more likely to be members of an ethnic minority. CCD's students are approximately 60 percent first-generation and 60 percent returning women. The college draws from metropolitan Denver, a city characterized by lower educational attainment levels among its citizens, more public school dropouts, more single parents, more welfare recipients, and higher levels of poverty among single parents and nuclear families than are recorded for any other area in the state.

One would not expect significant student achievement at the higher education level given these characteristics as a whole. Yet for 15 years students at CCD have been outperforming statewide averages, leading to the conclusion that these challenges to performance, singularly and collectively, are not insurmountable. CCD's responses to the challenges of diversity and preparedness—overwhelming odds—are examples of the power that great expectations and purposeful, positive change for improved student learning and student success can have on collegewide results.

Serious student needs and community problems are further exacerbated by funding cuts and significant limitations on what constituents in the community college service market can bear. Over the past decade, CCD's common goals and priorities have focused on cutting-edge issues such as diversity, technology, faculty development, and student learning. For the year 2000–01, the focus has shifted as a result of financial constraints within Colorado's higher education system. Along with most other North American community colleges, CCD faces reduced funding from traditional sources yet increased demands for services. CCD is trying to identify ways to balance its own needs as a quality institution with the options it has in the face of declining resources.

As we indicated in Chapter 1, the Community College of Denver has been recognized nationally and locally on multiple occasions for literally dozens of its successful programs, projects, and initiatives. These successes have occurred in spite of decreasing budgets and extraordinary student diversity. In this chapter, we showcase a representative number of this college's successful responses to its challenges.

CCD's Eyes on Success: Implementing Its Best Thinking

Numerous instructional components and special initiatives at CCD have received national and statewide recognition for their integral and critical roles in the institution's success. CCD's implementation of its best thinking about improving college teaching and student learning—thus, raising the levels of achievement for all students—is a study of the combined efforts of college administrators, faculty, and staff.

In this chapter, we examine

- CCD internal components critical to excellent instruction
- CCD scholarship programs for students
- CCD external partnerships and initiatives affecting the college and the community

These elements are key to CCD's success systems, the topic of the next chapter.

PROVIDING AND SUPPORTING TEACHING EXCELLENCE

Faculty and staff have agreed in writing to shared values for learning and to the critical thinking skills to develop across the curriculum. CCD has an established history of committing itself publicly to written objectives and goals, and these two principles—shared values for learning, and teaching critical skills—serve as the framework to discuss established components and initiatives.

SHARED VALUES FOR LEARNING

CCD faculty and staff are committed to a teaching/learning process that:

- Enables students to become independent learners
- Demonstrates a commitment to student outcomes (job readiness, computer literacy, skill levels, mastery of subject matters)
- Provides an opportunity for critical thinking and problem solving
- Demonstrates an excitement about teaching and learning
- Maintains high but realistic expectations
- Demonstrates an appreciation and an understanding of a diverse student population
- Practices an individualized, student-centered approach to encourage growth in student self-esteem

CRITICAL SKILLS ACROSS THE CURRICULUM

CCD faculty and administrators agree on the critical skills that must be taught and developed across the curriculum:

- Computation
- Computer literacy
- Reading
- Writing
- Speaking/listening
- Valuing diversity

We now turn to the programs and strategies that put these commitments into action.

THE ACADEMIC SUPPORT CENTER

The Academic Support Center (ASC), a multicultural, alternative learning environment, serves as a major retention resource for CCD by

- Providing a point of unity and support for all programs at the college
- Assisting students in clarifying and attaining their academic goals
- Facilitating communication between students and faculty
- Teaching students how to learn by focusing on each student's individual needs
- Giving students a sense of community and connection to the college
- Serving as an entry point and learning/teaching environment for students

Although the center provides an array of services for all CCD students, it is the key to the college's developmental program, according to faculty and staff alike. The centers houses a reading/study skills lab, math lab/writing lab/online writing lab (OWL), online math educator (MOLie), English as a second language, Special Learning Support Program (learning disabilities), Student Support Services (TRIO), and vocational tutoring services. Services also include a blend of one-on-one tutoring, small group work, and computer-assisted learning.

In 1989, the Colorado legislature mandated all precollege-level support services must be supplied by community colleges. CCD thus expanded its Academic Support Center to accommodate instruction in basic skills required of students attending CCD and its neighbor institutions, Metropolitan State College of Denver and the University of Colorado at Denver.

The expansion required moving ASC—along with all academic assistance programs—to a centrally located site on the Auraria Campus. This centralized location improved communication between similar programs, simplified referrals, reduced overlaps and redundancies in services, and created a one-stop center for academic need-based programs. ASC was situated close to the Educational Planning and Advising Center—the location for student enrollment, assessment, and advisement. Eventually the Vocational Tutoring Services component (formerly Supplemental Services) was added as well.

Initial funding came via a 1990 Title III grant designated for improving writing and math labs, implementing a Project Success program, and generating systemic program change. In 1993, ASC was awarded a second grant, which allowed for further program expansion, including the addition of Student Support Services and the Special Learning Support Program. ASC has expanded yet again, and now also serves all of the Technical Education Centers.

An unduplicated headcount reporting system documented more than 4,000 students used the center's services in one or more areas in fall 1999. Even after completing their developmental courses, students continue to use the ASC's assistance in college-level courses—some students coming from as far away as Boulder, Colorado. For many students, the lab environment serves as a safe haven—a comfort zone where they feel accepted and assured that they are receiving the support they need. While feeling the effects of these additional post-developmental students, the center's staff has avoided, thus far, placing restrictions on returning students. The word-of-mouth publicity, especially among English-as-a-second-language students, has successfully recruited many students to ASC. The online lab may have difficulty serving students if the current growth rate continues—in the interim, however, the ASC accommodates every student who comes through its doors.

Currently, the center operates with 14 employees—nine full-time and five with split assignments ranging from 20 to 80 percent of their workload. ASC also employs about 185 part-time tutors and technical support personnel. And, the center employs a full-time computer-aided instruction specialist for the purpose of training faculty, staff, and tutors in the most current technological advancements in education—which, in turn, is passed along to students. (While the lab experience provides an excellent training ground for tutors, this benefit also contributes to a high turnover among tutors who often secure higher-paying positions outside the college after completing their technical training.)

In the labs, full-time faculty, working split assignments, serve as coordinators to ensure that instructional and lab efforts are complimentary efforts. While it may be more cost-effective to hire part-time assistants to coordinate lab efforts, this is not a financial option. In Colorado, in order for a lab to earn full-time-equivalency funds, it must be under direct faculty supervision.

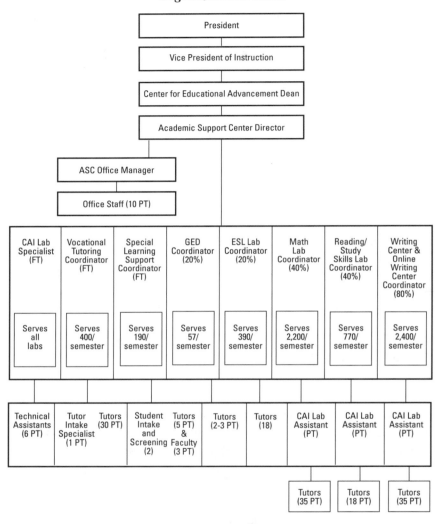

Figure 3.1 Community College of Denver Academic Support Center Organizational Chart

Although not mental health specialists, the ASC faculty, staff, and tutors recognize that they cannot separate the mental health issues that learning, psychological, economic, or physical difficulties create for students and the quality of the instructional services they provide in the lab. For this reason, many students who are involved with lab experiences as part of their assigned program of study will continue to return to CCD's labs, either for assistance or to work as tutors, throughout their college experience (whether they are at CCD or in a regional four-year college or university).

ASC labs and its students form symbiotic partnerships. Financially, students view ASC as an academic bargain—providing critical assessment and tutoring services that many could not afford anywhere else. Personally, many students report they want to repay the system that has supported them academically and appreciate any opportunities to work as peer tutors in that environment. Students who complete their training as peer tutors and begin their work with students in the ASC labs discover that the tutoring experience continues to strengthen their own self-esteem and academic confidence, and provides continuing support for their own learning.

As many of CCD's urban, adult population juggle family, work, and college responsibilities, customer service and facility convenience are major considerations. Being centrally located on the Auraria Campus is an accessibility plus situation for the ASC labs—they are accessible to students during day and evening hours, as well as on Saturdays. To raise the level of customer convenience, ASC brought instructional technology directly into the lab, saving students valuable time searching for a computer elsewhere on campus.

FINANCING

The operating budget for ASC relies heavily on grant requisitions. During the grant application process, the center's staff works closely with CCD's Institutional Advancement team. The 1993 TRIO grant is an excellent example of this collaborative effort. Historically, only four-year institutions could apply and receive TRIO funding; recently, community colleges can compete as well. To maintain its competitiveness and to be considered for the fifth year of the grant, a college must demonstrate exemplary performance during its first four years. Fewer than 10 percent of all eligible programs nationwide have received the five-year award. CCD was one of the few community colleges awarded five-year grants.

OUTCOME DATA

In 1998, ASC installed a new database tracking system. New data indicate that students receiving ASC services for three or more hours per week have a success rate of 90 to 92 percent, depending on program and lab access. Further analysis of these data reveals the class withdrawal rate for students receiving ASC support is 7.75 percent, compared with 12.37 for the overall CCD campus rate. CCD students who do not use ASC have a withdrawal rate of 25 percent. Because the ASC withdrawal rate is included in CCD's overall rate, ASC reports "it is reasonable to assume that students who are helped by the ASC withdraw about 50 percent less often than students who do not receive this assistance."

Graduation rates are similarly affected. CCD's graduation rates have doubled from 17.5 percent to 35.1 percent, indicating a correlation between the increase in support services and the number of CCD graduates. All areas report success rates in the 80 and 90 percentile range, except for the GED program, which reports an impressive 70 percent success rate.

THE LAB EXPERIENCE

Tutors work closely with students on a day-to-day basis and are viewed as the critical link in open, honest communication between the support staff and the student. There are three types of tutor positions available at ASC: peer, new professional, and professional.

Peer tutors have completed a minimum of two or three college-level courses in the discipline to be tutored, are new to tutoring, and have earned less than a bachelor's degree. Labs and program peer tutors need a recommendation from a content area instructor and require training and support from more experienced staff.

New professional tutors have attained at least a bachelor's degree or the equivalent in their field. They have less than two years of teaching/tutoring experience. Training and support are considered key components in assuring tutoring success.

Professional tutors have attained a minimum of a bachelor's degree or the equivalent with more than two years of teaching/tutoring experience. They are able to mentor less experienced tutors; can solve students' difficulties; work independently with students; and are qualified to function as lead tutors in labs. Lead tutors assist in the day-to-day functioning of the labs for additional compensation.

Both peer tutors and new professional tutors are required to attend general training sessions during their first semester of employment. Training workshops comprise an overview of Academic Support Center and Auraria (campus) services; reinforcing study skills when tutoring; and using computer-aided instruction in tutoring. Tutors are evaluated every fall semester by their students; full-time faculty tutors are evaluated both fall and spring semesters. Evaluations ask about specific behaviors exhibited by the tutors and about students' future interests in tutoring sessions: "The tutor listens to me and understands my concerns," "The tutor helps me to do the work instead of doing the work for me," and "The tutor is someone I would work with again." Evaluations are made on a 5.0 scale, ranging from Outstanding (4.5–5.0) to Unsatisfactory (1.0–1.49). Tutor ratings are consistently high, most recently averaging a remarkable 4.79.

Developmental education students often experience problems in multiple areas. Rather than one formal meeting each week to discuss student and program issues, ASC program coordinators meet informally every day to discuss concerns. Being centrally located helps keep communication lines open, encourages a team approach to problem solving, and stops students from falling through cracks in the system.

When students enter an ASC program, the first step is to determine the appropriate level of basic skill instruction they should receive. Today's ASC labs serve more as a support system for the various developmental education courses instead of a delivery point for instruction (except in the case of GED instruction). The center houses a variety of student services categorized as either lab tutoring services or student support programs. Tutoring programs include instruction for the GED, ESL, mathematics, reading/study skills, Special Learning Support, and writing. In every case, students have opportunities to expand their instruction by individual and/or group tutoring, computer tutorials, course videos, and instructional workshops.

ASC uses a comprehensive process for reporting students' use of lab materials and services. Culling information from lab sign-in sheets, ASC regularly distributes reports to all support labs detailing individual hourly usage. In addition, the various support programs—such as Vocational Tutoring Services—provide every discipline center with additional progress reports documenting the use of its program services. Serving as an early alert system, the various ASC reports let faculty and support staff know about student problems, including poor lab attendance.

PROJECT SUCCESS DAY
Another special support service is Project Success Day, a daylong opportunity for students to visit with faculty and support services staff about their academic progress. Designed to identify students who need extra help early in the semester, Project Success Day occurs both fall and spring semesters, during the first quarter of the term. In preparation for the

event, ASC distributes class rosters to all faculty, who then note every student's attendance, academic progress, and suggestions for academic assistance. ASC then scans these rosters and prepares personalized progress reports for each student, indicating his or her academic standing and offering information about Project Success Day, available lab services, and special college resources. Armed with this information, students can attend Project Success Day and visit with prospective tutors and lab staff without feeling singled out or pressured.

ADVISING DAY

Another special support effort is Advising Day, which occurs mid-semester in the fall and spring. Faculty and advisers meet with students to review their academic progress and plan for the upcoming semester. Faculty and students discuss not only course selection but career paths, study strategies, assistance available, and barriers to education. Faculty and advisers may also help students apply to programs of their choice. Moreover, they serve as mentors to students, actively communicating concerns and recommendations to them prior to Project Success and Advising Days.

THE SPECIAL LEARNING SUPPORT PROGRAM

The Special Learning Support Program offers academic assistance or specific accommodations to students with learning disabilities or special learning needs. Even with reduced funding over the past several years, this program continues to offer the most comprehensive community college learning disabilities program in Colorado, complete with program coordinator and special classes for learning-disabled students. Some students enter this program having completed a formal learning-disability evaluation process, but many cannot afford this screening process and arrive without even baseline information by which staff members can design a useful support program. Therefore, while the Special Learning Support Program staff cannot provide the full range of evaluative and diagnostic procedures, they do administer basic diagnostic tests to help identify the major learning problems from which they can make assignments in proper learning techniques and accommodations.

When the evaluation process is complete, the student is advised about course placement: The student has the option of accepting the proposed recommendations or signing a waiver, releasing the college from future academic liability. A student's reluctance to participate usually occurs in response to some misconceptions about learning disability classes, or because they believe they will be successful in college courses without the special instruction. Those students who elect to take the program receive specialized classes in spelling, mathematics, reading, writing, and study skills; and there are classroom and testing accommodations, including books on tape, note takers, and extended test time.

Throughout the program, students receive extensive academic, financial aid, and personal counseling to support their academic needs. As does ASC, the Special Learning Support Program finds that many students continue to return to the labs long after they have finished their program of study and are enrolled in college-level courses at CCD or surrounding four-year institutions.

STUDENT SUPPORT SERVICES

As a member of the TRIO branch of federally funded programs, CCD's Student Support Services (SSS) program is designed to assist low-income, first-generation college students and/or students with disabilities. TRIO programs began as part of President Lyndon Johnson's War on Poverty in the 1960s. In the beginning, the Upward Bound and Educational Talent Search focused primarily on middle and high school students interested in pursuing a college education, while Student Support Services directed its efforts toward assisting college students. Today, all three Auraria Campus institutions (CCD, MSCD, and UCD) support SSS programs. In addition, Metropolitan State College supports a Veterans' Upward Bound program, and CCD supports a Talent Search program.

Initially, TRIO was designed to assist first-generation students of color; but eligibility standards changed from a minority focus to an all-inclusive, low-income/disability focus. Unfortunately, while today a student might meet the qualifications of first-generation, low-income, and disabled, he or she will be disqualified if there is no documented academic need.

Most SSS program funding comes from federal grant monies, but CCD provides additional support, such as in-kind contributions of office space, telephones, and duplicating services. TRIO provides local program coordinators with intensive training and a network support system using state, regional, and national organizations. In addition to being involved in the Colorado state organization, the SSS program coordinator has the option of seeking assistance from one of the 10 regional organizations, which, in turn, is accountable to the Council for Opportunities in Education in

Washington, D.C. In large part, the program's 30-year history is a direct result of successful professional networking.

The program has a small staff. The program coordinator is responsible for project peer mentoring and counseling. The program employs an administrative assistant who monitors all grant accounting, an academic case manager who oversees all project tutoring, 10 to 12 peer mentors, and eight or more tutors. The mentors, hired either on a work-study or study-hourly basis, often are products of the program and possess strong, interpersonal communication skills—especially critical when working with at-risk students.

Although the program is designed for 200 students per grant year, the 1998–99 program enrollment topped more than 240. Program recruiting is prohibited, but students often learn about the program by word-of-mouth from other students, faculty, or institutions. Sometimes, either the advising or financial aid office will refer students to this program.

Following acceptance into the program, a student is required to attend an orientation session with his case manager. The case manager will explain the program's objectives to the student and write an Individualized Educational Plan for tracking student progress. Unlike many student assistance programs where sporadic attendance is acceptable, SSS program attendance is monitored closely. Students have a wealth of services available to them including academic advising, career counseling, tutoring, financial aid and transfer assistance, and cultural events.

The program is successful, as shown by these statistics. The program currently reports an 88 percent success rate and includes both continuing students and transferring/graduating students. The college retains more than 80 percent of SSS students each year. Over 80 percent of SSS students maintain at least a 2.0 GPA; in fact, about half have a 3.0 GPA or higher. About 75 percent of SSS students who are eligible to graduate and/or transfer do so each year.

The program provides students with the critical elements or successful retention, including case management, one-on-one student contact, and college connections. Many faculty and staff connected to this program observed that the program's real strength is in its inter-connections with other ASC programs: the financial and advising offices, the Student Assistance Center, the Center for Students with Disabilities, and CCD faculty.

Summer Bridge Program

For more than a decade, the Summer Bridge Program has reached into the CCD service area to assist local high school students as they prepare for college. The programs also targets students who are 17 to 22 years of age; who have dropped out or stopped and need only a few credits to graduate; and/or who did not formerly make college a first option but now have an interest in improving their basic skills, exploring career options, and declaring a preliminary major. Since the bridge program is under SSS direction, program participants have an immediate connection to academic support upon enrolling in CCD. Although Summer Bridge serves as a recruitment initiative for the SSS program, participants receive information on a variety of higher education options including two-year, two-year transfer, and four-year options. The program's primary purpose is to help students begin to see themselves in higher education.

Vocational Tutoring Services

Formerly called Supplemental Services, CCD's Vocational Tutoring Services (VTS) program has been assisting vocational program students for almost three decades. Originating in 1974 and federally funded through Colorado's Community College and Occupational Educational System, the VTS program provides students with a variety of basic skills, ESL, and vocational tutoring options. These options include one-on-one, small group, and lab-supported tutoring. Dedicated to assisting all student populations, VTS actively involves students in the learning process and strongly encourages them to become independent learners. Serving in an advocacy role, VTS personnel assist students with referrals and interactions involving outside employers once a student has declared a vocational major.

In addition to being a CCD student with a declared vocational major or concentration, a potential VTS candidate must possess an academic need or learning disability. For final qualifying purposes, a student must seek an instructor's, counselor's, or college official's assistance in completing a student profile and needs assessment. Since student success is a top priority, VTS case managers regularly coordinate efforts with other ASC program personnel to guarantee quality student service and effective spending of program dollars.

Summer 1998 to spring 1999 data indicate a 95 percent success rate among the more than 890 students served. A March 2000 midyear progress report indicates a total of 749 students being served and an

87 percent success rate. This number includes students who are academically and economically disadvantaged, as well as many with limited English proficient.

THE DEVELOPMENTAL EDUCATION PROGRAM

CCD has the largest number and percentages of students in developmental courses in the state; it has the largest number of multiple developmental course takers; and 37 percent of its people of color are enrolled in developmental courses (CCD 1997–98 data). The diversity of CCD's student body—and the characteristics that put them most at risk in achieving academic success—has compelled administrators, faculty, and staff to design and implement a strong developmental education component as a required feature of the college curriculum. President McClenney, who has a long history of advocacy for remedial and developmental programs, identifies developmental education as a critical point of entry to the college for students needing basic skills and maintains that its programs and faculty deserve and will receive equal status with others that traditionally have been identified as college level.

The majority of variables within CCD's formula for success are linked to developmental education and to building a strong academic foundation. Since its early 1970s beginning, CCD's developmental education program has undergone several major organizational transformations ranging from lab only, to developmental classes and lab, to reorganization under the auspices of a centralized developmental studies division. With CCD's new instructional reorganization, all developmental education services were gathered under the Center for Educational Advancement to improve communication and coordination between available services, including instruction in reading, precollegiate English, precollegiate mathematics, English as a second language, general equivalency diploma, and services through the Test Center, Academic Support Center, and GED institutes (throughout Denver). Developmental education at the branch campuses (TECs) is implemented in basic skills labs, self-paced classes with open entry and open exit, and the intervention model, using case managers. Similar to past restructuring efforts where college finances drove institutional change, the 1999 reorganization efforts were designed to improve the financial efficiency and instructional effectiveness of remedial education, which in turn links directly to CCD's student success rates. As a result of improved communication among faculty, staff, and students, all CCD students encounter less bureaucracy and fewer learning obstacles.

The Center for Educational Advancement provides an array of remedial courses and support services. While small class size plays a vital role in the student success formula, it is the combination of developmental course work and support services that provide students with confidence and improved self-esteem to continue their college studies. Students are monitored closely by the college's high-tech, high-touch student approach—clearly evident at the TEC sites and in the Academic Support Center's programs, where self-directed learning and a case manager model are used. In addition, lab usage reports, Project Success Day, Advising Day, and the Summer Bridge Program serve as additional academic safety nets to ensure students are prepared adequately to face the rigors of higher education.

For students enrolled in developmental courses, learning is enhanced further by the one-hour-a-week lab requirement and the one-on-one faculty, mentor, or tutor contact procedure. For many first-generation students, this personal contact is essential for learning basic skills, study skills, and time management techniques, as well as the culture of the institution.

Often, the lab setting provides a surrogate family environment, offering the nurturing support missing in many students' lives. Dialogue sessions—often triggered by student stories conveyed through developmental writing assignments, for example—provide excellent opportunities for students to talk about problems and frustrations, and for staff members to get to know students better.

A quarter century of experimentation has led CCD's administration and developmental education division to conclude that a centralized focus would best serve the college's large number of at-risk, skill-deficient students. Although students participating in centralized developmental education programs experience higher success and retention rates than students in more decentralized programs (Roueche and Roueche 1999), many nationally recognized community colleges with embedded or decentralized models also report high student success levels. Therefore, the critical decision any college should make is not so much about implementing a specific model but rather a blend of factors that in combination form a conducive learning environment for student success.

CCD tracks student success in order to evaluate programs and strategies. Institutionally, the college reached a milestone in 1998–99 when more than 50 percent of its graduates and transfers were students of color (in 1985–86 it was 13 percent). People of color make up approximately

35 percent of the adult population in the CCD service area yet approximately 60 percent of CCD's developmental course enrollees. One of the most compelling data reports was that fall-to-fall semester retention for students starting their college work in developmental courses was between 50 and 60 percent from 1993 to 1997, and the cumulative GPA of first-time developmental students who finished one full year at CCD stood at 2.94 (in a 4.0 system). Another report documented that developmental students who took English composition had a 71.7 percent success rate and a 75.6 percent success rate in college algebra—two courses many faculty agree are gateways to successful experiences in subsequent courses in the majority of college programs.

Table 3.1 Percentage of Community College of Denver Students Actively Engaged in Developmental Education, 1997–98

Measure	Percentage
Head-count enrollment in developmental courses as a percentage of total enrollment	44%
Percentage of first-time enrollees who enroll in developmental courses	52%
Percentage of developmental course enrollees who are full-time students	26%
Percentage of developmental course enrollees who are women	58%
Percentage of developmental course enrollees who are people of color	59.3%
Percentage of developmental students with course completions in 1997–98	72%
Fall-to-fall retention for students starting in developmental courses	50–60%
Percentage of students enrolled in ESL	9%
Fall-to-fall retention of ESL students (1993 to 1997)	57.1–75%

Table 3.1a Subsequent Success of Developmental Students

Course	Percentage Passing
English composition	71.7%
College algebra	75.6%

THE SERVICE LEARNING CENTER

Since opening in 1994, CCD's Service Learning Center (SLC) has proved that learning need not be limited to the classroom. Service learning staff seek experiences incorporating community service, academic instruction, and students' critical thinking abilities into a unique learning format. SLC's primary purpose is "to enhance the student experience through the integration of academic study and service in order to encourage civic involvement, community service, and responsible leadership." To assist students with community job placement, the center maintains a database of participating community businesses and agencies, linking students and organizations via essential orientation materials, and assists faculty with syllabi, curriculum development, and service learning resource material.

As mentioned earlier, CCD has long-term working relationships with community organizations; the college fosters student interest and involvement in community development, as well. Students take their classroom learning into the community and bring their community work experiences back into the classroom for analysis. A critical link in the experiential learning process, service learning makes students think critically about their community experiences, be actively involved in applying what they learn to real-world situations, and come to value work and classroom experiences simultaneously. Service learning gives students on-the-job training in potential careers, and also allows the students to make valuable community contacts and expand their opportunities for future employment. Moreover, service learning can be done on campus for students to work with college programs needing various services.

In 1998, approximately 48 students participated in service learning projects; during 1999–2000, this number rose to 300. The current database of community partners lists more than 200 businesses and organizations— past, present, and future employers of service learners. In addition, 10 on-campus programs are active recruiters of service learning students. Student retention rates and academic achievement levels are improved in part as a result of students' service learning experiences as shown by data analysis done for program evaluation. Informal data also indicate that students will self-select a service learning course above and beyond their regular class load when their choices of courses for a given semester does not include a service learning option.

The Service Learning program publishes a fall, spring, and summer newsletter, *the snooz*. This publication is distributed across CCD campuses to encourage student participation in service learning, announce events and opportunities for service learning experiences, and recognize outstanding student service to learning projects. In addition, the college learning Web site contains projects, sites, and contacts for service learning, as well as anecdotes from students who participated in service learning.

THE TEACHING/LEARNING CENTER

The quality of instruction at this college depends on the faculty who tend to its organization, its methods, and its results. CCD concern for its students is matched by its concern for its faculty. CCD makes sure faculty have multiple opportunities to fine-tune their teaching skills, identify and implement appropriate instructional technologies, and stay current in their fields.

CCD recognizes the critical role that faculty and staff support services play in keeping the instructors doing their best and on the cutting edge of their profession. Established to offer quality professional development for faculty and staff and to further the institutional goal of improving student performance, the Teaching/Learning Center (T/LC) provides affordable, high-quality, in-house professional development services.

From its inception, the T/LC has been growing into a highly visible, respected, essential college unit. Early on, the center played an instrumental role in establishing the college's Shared Values for Teaching Excellence, thereby implementing critical skills across the curriculum. T/LC also developed the Critical Skills Handbook and individual course content guides. T/LC supports and encourages learning community and service learning innovations. Promoting valuing diversity events and training also fell into T/LC's bailiwick. More recently, the center has worked closely with faculty to design an institutional credentialing policy and a pay-for-performance plan for full-time faculty. Today, T/LC leads many initiatives as the college evolves from a teaching to a learning college. T/LC hosts 125 workshops annually addressing faculty orientation and organizational culture; advising and retention strategies; teaching, learning, and classroom management techniques; curriculum development; and technology and valuing diversity training. As an added incentive, the T/LC awards mini-grants to faculty to pursue an innovative or creative project of benefit to CCD teaching/learning environment (*CCD Facts 1998–99*). Mini-grant proposals must be tied directly to the college's action priorities. Following project completion, all grant recipients share their project experiences and results with the college community through a series of workshops. Growing its own expertise rewards not only CCD faculty, but also the college; shared growth raises the performance levels for all college components.

T/LC has developed ready reference materials on such topics as learning styles, diversity, electronic media, course content guides, academic Web-based resources, and online tutoring. These materials assist instructors in developing a solid planning process and encouraging and stimulating innovative classroom activities.

T/LC uses a significant amount of its professional development time to train instructors on the electronic media's versatility in course preparation, presentations, faculty-student communications, assessment, and grading. With distance learning on the increase, T/LC works directly with faculty to ensure quality online course and support services. Unfortunately, CCD's ability to remain technologically current is affected by college budgetary constraints; the college is constantly seeking outside funding and equipment requisition sources.

To keep abreast of changing professional development and support needs, T/LC periodically surveys faculty and staff. New staff development opportunities are then created to meet the college's changing needs. The center also conducts periodic evaluations to ascertain whether or not it is meeting the needs of its community.

T/LC operates as a nucleus for change and leads the college in its efforts to become a learning college. As a catalyst, the center gets its direction from the college's action priorities and from the local community; then it develops an education and training plan to achieve the priorities plan.

In Chapter 2, we cited CCD's March 2000 honor as recipient of the Hesburgh Award, given in recognition of the most outstanding professional development program in higher education. This award specifically recognizes a program within an institution, but it is given to the institution and received by its president. The Teaching/Learning Center was the program recognized with the Hesburgh Award; President McClenney and the CCD T/LC director and dean of the Center for Learning Outreach, Dianne Cyr, were at the ceremony. One of 62 community and four-year colleges and universities considered for this prestigious award, CCD is the only community college ever to receive this recognition.

ADDITIONAL FUNDING SOURCES SUPPORTING STUDENT SUCCESS

Typical of the national trends among community colleges, CCD is experiencing tremendous budgetary restrictions and constraints. Underfunded—both compared with other community colleges in Colorado and nationally—CCD seeks additional external resources to fund its mission activities. One source of outside funding is grants. In 1999, the La Familia Scholars Program received a fourth consecutive year of funding from the U.S. Department of Education; the Work and Family Resource Center received grants in excess of $400,000; the Welfare-to-Work efforts received $440,000 in grants; and Continuing Education received $140,000 from Colorado First/Existing Industry grants. CCD also works collaboratively to raise money. A $1.4 million technology grant for Information Resources and Planning—in cooperation with several community partners—created numerous technology projects. The CCD Technical Education Centers, in collaboration with the Denver Mayor's Office of Employment and Training (MOET) and other community partners, received approval for a $2 million Youth Opportunity Grant. CCD also receives scholarship money for individual students. CCD's Financial Aid Department managed more than $8 million in student aid funds assisting more than 4,445 students during the 1998–99 school year. Some programs and projects deserve special mention for the boost they have given CCD: the President's First Generation Scholarship Program, La Familia Scholars Program, and "Drive for Education" Scholarships.

PRESIDENT'S FIRST GENERATION SCHOLARSHIP PROGRAM

The President's First Generation Scholarship (PFGS) Program is designed to help individuals become their families' first college graduate. Applicants must be residents of Colorado and neither parent(s) nor guardian may have earned a four-year college degree. The only program of its kind among Colorado community colleges, PFGS gives scholars financial assistance and other resources to support their studies toward associate and baccalaureate degrees. Program activities include mentoring, academic workshops and leadership seminars, community service seminars and community-building activities, service-learning experiences, and transfer opportunities to private and public four-year colleges and universities in Colorado (CCD currently has eight formal transfer agreements).

A committee of faculty and staff selects students based on financial need and cumulative high school grade point averages at graduation (2.5 and higher, or comparable GED test scores). Selection criteria do not include ethnicity, gender, or age; recipients reflect a broad demographic profile. Students must maintain a minimum grade point average of 2.5 to retain scholarship status.

Regular PFGS evaluations include surveys of the scholarship recipients, feedback from members of the community external to the college, and input from CCD faculty and staff. Once scholarship recipients have left the program, CCD's Information Resources and Planning Department tracks their activities—including the programs they enter and their progress in those courses. The collected data are used to improve the program's selection process and activities.

College data document the success of PFGS. The 1999–2000 PFGS cohort includes 32 students. Fourteen of the 21 scholars beginning fall 1996 completed spring 1997 with a 3.0 GPA or higher; 21 of 28 scholars who attended in fall 1997 earned a cumulative GPA of 3.0 or higher (14 of the 28 earned 3.5 or higher; 2 of the 28 earned 4.0).

Currently, the PFGS program is funded by contributions from CCD faculty, staff, and alumni; seven Denver area companies and organizations; several major corporate foundations; and one private estate donation in memory of a former CCD student. Investments in this program defray the costs of tuition and fees for scholarship recipients and cover all administrative costs associated with the program.

La Familia

The La Familia (The Family) Scholars Program is built on the model of a Latino "family culture," intended to create an environment supportive for first-generation Spanish-speaking students' academic, social, technological, and personal needs. In addition to other course work, each student enrolls in a six-hour learning community class combining technology, education and career planning, and learning skills. The learning community classes are conducted in a state-of-the-art computerized classroom, and students also have access to a computerized lab for tutor and computer support. The project's faculty and staff work closely with CCD's Academic Support Center to help ensure student success and improve retention and graduation rates.

A solid example of successful interdisciplinary learning communities, the La Familia Scholars Program integrates two or more courses into a single course design. Students not only have the benefit of developing multiple skills but the advantage of having multiple instructor assistance for six-hour blocks of time. All learning community curriculum is embedded with the mandated critical skills of math reasoning, reading, writing, speaking, valuing diversity, and computer technology. Collaboration has been identified as the critical consideration for program longevity; student success receives priority consideration.

La Familia scholars also have case managers and peer mentors who serve as advisers and provide information about classes and programs.

The La Familia staff works with CCD administrators, faculty, and staff to help these new students adapt to college life and improve their chances of persisting to an associate's degree. Community members, high school counselors, and baccalaureate institutions' support staffs also participate in support activities. Currently, the project reports an 80 percent retention rate for 250 students annually and an average 86 percent first-to-second semester retention rate for Latino students.

In addition to increasing CCD's 1998–99 graduation rate by 9 percent, the project also contributed to the college's record-breaking 20 percent Latino graduation rate. While more than 80 percent of the students participating in learning community reading classes achieved a grade of C or higher, program graduates overall scored above average on all Academic Profile norm-reference exams. In a 1999 survey, 96 percent of La Familia's Latino student population reported their culture was valued and the encouragement of the learning community's faculty influenced their decisions to complete their education (P. Valdez-Ferguson, personal communication, April 2000).

This project, funded by a U.S. Department of Education Title III grant designated for Hispanic-Serving Institutions, has been featured in the *Chronicle of Higher Education* and *Hispanic Outlook* and in a national teleconference entitled "Transformational Change within Community Colleges"; it has also been identified as a "model of transformational change that has the potential to create systemic change and to strengthen the institution" (P. Valdez-Ferguson, personal communication, April 2000). CCD is one of 128 Hispanic-Serving Institutions in the United States; grant guidelines require that Latino students represent more than 25 percent of the total student body (CCD's Latino student population is approximately 30 percent).

Latino first-generation students are given priority when they apply to the program, but then other students are accepted until enrollment limits are met. Students accepted into La Familia Scholars Program must be first-generation college attendees, and neither parent(s) nor guardian(s) may possess a high school diploma or a GED certificate. Although not always mandated, low-income students will be given priority status at the time of application.

Scholarships supported by a fixed dollar amount set aside upon the purchase of any vehicle from any John Elway dealership were available in 1997–98 and 1998–99. Selection criteria required that the student

- Be a resident of and graduate from a public school located in one of six Colorado counties in the Denver metropolitan area
- Be a U.S. citizen
- Have attained a minimum cumulative GPA of 2.6 in high school
- Be enrolled in an eligible institution for a minimum of 12 hours each semester
- Demonstrate financial need (appropriate for CCD's population and approved by the dealerships)
- Demonstrate a history of community involvement and good citizenship (best effort)
- Be a full-time student at CCD
- Apply for all other potential scholarship funds (as the "Drive for Education" Scholarships are meant to be last dollars)

The scholarships provided $375 per semester per recipient, and CCD provided a dollar-for-dollar matching contribution. In addition, CCD provided the dealerships with year-end performance reports for each recipient.

COMMUNITY PARTNERSHIPS AND INITIATIVES

CCD's numerous partnerships and initiatives with external entities increase demand for college programs and services, and simultaneously help support them. These collaborations demonstrate CCD's keen interest in active, broad-based involvement in community and economic development. Ultimately, they underscore the critical nature of return on investment—the college has become a working partner who believes in giving back to its community, and the community has responded with active appreciation for CCD's commitments and support.

THE DENVER EDUCATION NETWORK

The Denver Education Network, under CCD's direction, works to provide a seamless system of educational services for local K–12 urban students. Viewed as a retention strategy, the Denver Education Network is a retention strategy aimed at reducing the urban dropout rate at all educational levels.

In fall 1991, Steve Zwerling and other representatives from the Ford Foundation met with President McClenney to suggest that Ford would support education reform in Denver via the Denver Network, a collaborative of public schools and other entities and individuals from public and private sectors of the community. Since its inception in 1991, the Denver Education Network has worked with local community organizations and schools to enable Denver-area students to attain postsecondary degrees.

The Denver Education Network continues to seek new and improved methods to help students succeed. The Ford Foundation has encouraged creative thinking, risk taking, and program experimentation without the fear of penalty, in the interest of making a positive difference in education and in the lives of students. The Ford Foundation underwrites the Urban Partnership Project, a national network of local and regional organizations dedicated to accepting local responsibility for educating all children. The Denver Education Network is the local affiliate for the Urban Partnership Project; as such, it receives support from the Ford Foundation and through it linkages to similar efforts nationwide (Taber 1995). Ford requires sufficient local and regional buy-in to continue its support.

To improve high school and higher education graduation rates, the Denver Education Network has assisted local elementary, middle, and high school students by coordinating regular college visits to familiarize them with the campus environment and by working with the students and their parents on the college application and financial aid processes. Once a student has been accepted to CCD, the Denver Education Network serves in a mentoring capacity, contacting students on a regular basis and linking students to various campus support services as needed.

While most program funding comes directly from Ford Foundation grant monies, CCD and the president's office give addition support and in-kind assistance. The 10-year grant funding is coming to a close, so the Denver Education Network program coordinator is working closely with CCD's Institutional Advancement division to secure new money to continue the program.

COMPUTER TRAINING FOR PEOPLE WITH DISABILITIES

Established in 1981, the Computer Training for People with Disabilities program is one of approximately 35 programs initiated by IBM still operating in the United States and Canada. The program resulted from a partnership among the business community, the Colorado Department of Vocational Rehabilitation, and CCD. In 1993, the Colorado Commission on Higher Education designated the Computer Training for People with Disabilities a "Program of Excellence." Its purpose is to meet the needs of the business community for competent computer programmers and network administrators, as well as the needs of injured workers and people with disabilities for challenging, lifelong careers.

The job outlook is bright; over the past 17 years, more than 90 percent for each class has secured jobs. Starting salaries for the 1998 graduating class ranged from $35,000 to $43,000. Many employers seek potential employees at CCD. The graduates take CCD's competencies guarantees with them: Because CCD guarantees its associate degree and certificate programs, if the employer finds the graduate lacks skills required for employment (field-specific skills), the graduate receives up to nine free credit hours at CCD to increase student competency.

The students selected into this program are motivated and able to learn in an accelerated educational environment. A seven-to-nine-week internship in industry follows 11 months of academic training. The final semester of work includes a capstone course that reviews and assesses students' competencies in computers or allows the student to participate in a cooperative education experience to enhance competencies. Program goals include producing graduates with these characteristics:

- Highly motivated
- Positive attitude
- Well-adjusted to disability or injury
- Aptitude for problem solving
- Tolerance for an 8- to 10-hour day
- Positive employment and academic history

THE HISPANIC INSTITUTE

CCD's first effort to focus on the needs of its community was the Colorado Institute for Hispanic Education and Economic Development. Funded by CCD, Metropolitan State College, and the University of Colorado at Denver (all three institutions share a campus known as the Auraria Higher

Education Center, located in downtown Denver), CCD served as host and fiscal agent. The institute began during 1987–88, led by a community board and an executive director. Its most successful projects include a leadership development effort that now boasts more than 200 alumni, the creation of the Small Business Development Center, and the Denver Education Network.

THE COLORADO CAMPUS COMPACT

A coalition of 21 Colorado presidents representing state, public, and private universities and colleges, the Colorado Campus Compact creates public service opportunities for students and encourages faculty to include service learning in undergraduate courses and programs. CCD's Service Learning Center is described in this chapter.

These three collaborative efforts—Denver Education Network, Hispanic Institute, and Colorado Campus Compact—share these special characteristics:

- Use of a community board or steering committee to lead the effort
- Employment of a full-time professional director
- Multiple funding agents (each of the partners contributes some type of resources)
- Hosted by the Community College of Denver (Roueche, Taber, and Roueche 1995, 86–87)

DENVER FAMILY OPPORTUNITY

Of its numerous collaborative efforts, President McClenney cites the Denver Family Opportunity Program (DFO) as having the greatest impact on his community. In 1988, Denver's mayor invited McClenney to chair the DFO's governing council as it tackled reform efforts to improve Denver's welfare program—specifically, to stimulate self-sufficiency among recipients of support from Aid to Families with Dependent Children. CCD has continued to be involved in this effort, with more than 500 welfare recipients enrolled in certificate and degree programs at any given time. CCD's strong relationships with the Denver Department of Social Services and numerous community-based organizations involved in welfare reform efforts have led to various other partnerships—for example, case managers and human services agents routinely refer clients to CCD's TEC training programs.

In addition to these initiatives and partnerships, CCD remains involved with the Denver public elementary, middle, and high schools by:

- Providing enrichment programs for Denver Independent School District students to allow their parents to take English as a second language and adult basic education courses on the school campuses nearby
- Conducting sessions in the high schools—beginning with ninth-grade students and their families—to emphasize the critical need to continue beyond high school and to complete the appropriate high school courses to prepare for college work
- Annually increasing the number of Denver Independent School District graduates who enroll in CCD courses and programs by establishing a major presence in Denver's K–12 public education system

Moreover, CCD continues to strengthen an "opportunity" presence in housing projects and other off-campus locations by offering literacy classes and other adult education activities and courses at times and in places convenient to recipients of welfare and to other Denver citizens afflicted by unemployment, low income, and low levels of educational attainment.

CONCLUSIONS

More than a decade ago, *Access and Excellence: The Open-Door College* (Roueche and Baker 1987) focused on one institution's ability to balance equity of access with academic excellence. Based upon a national study of community colleges' policies, programs, and outcomes, the researchers identified systems for success that created the most fertile ground for the successful balance of open access and educational excellence. They chose to showcase Miami-Dade Community College's (Fla.) policies and procedures that promoted retention and achievement with great success in a highly diverse student body. Today, we are looking again at these fertile grounds, and the Community College of Denver meets all of the criteria used to describe another extraordinarily successful college. CCD, working against the odds, has implemented a balanced combination of leadership, instruction, community, and climate to keep the door open and college programs at high levels of quality.

CCD has a collaborative environment supporting organizational and educational excellence. Its own reform movements—agreed upon by, faculty and staff—account for the majority of its extraordinary results. The list of CCD accomplishments with which we close this chapter could not have occurred without its unique climate for learning, administrative leadership, teaching excellence, and foundation of support systems spanning and linking all college components.

The CCD message is spelled out on the college's Web site—www. rightchoice.org—and in its *CCD Facts* booklet. CCD's most recent report on its Measurements of Success, *CCD—Demonstrating Excellence through Accountability*, lists the following achievements:

- Between 1987 and 1998, CCD increased the total number of graduates by 81 percent.
- Between 1987 and 1998, people of color as a percent of total graduates more than doubled—from 20 percent to 45.6 percent.
- Between 1987 and 1998, CCD nearly quadrupled the number of graduates of color, from 83 to 318 graduates.
- Between 1992 and 1996 nine out of every ten CCD graduates who applied for transfer were accepted into Colorado four-year public colleges and universities.*
- The average cumulative grade point average of CCD transfer graduates in 1995–96 at four-year schools was 2.9 on a 4.0 scale.**
- Of 1996–97 graduates, 95 percent were satisfied with their CCD educational program.
- Of 1998 currently enrolled students, 98 percent were satisfied with the instruction they had received.
- Every employer surveyed in 1996 was satisfied with the skills of CCD graduates.

*In 1997, acceptance rates of Community College of Denver graduate applicants to Colorado four-year public institutions was 92.3 (CCCOES Educational Support Services from CCHE SURDS extract file, 2/12/99).

**1996–97, the grade point average was 3.0 on a 4.0 scale (CCCOES Education Support Services from CCHE SURDS extract file—12 February 1999).

In this chapter, we have described some of the components of the Community College of Denver's success. They have been tested over time and can be adapted or adopted by other institutions that seek to achieve that critical balance of access and excellence. We now turn from some of the programs, partnerships, and support strategies that have earned CCD widespread recognition and acclaim and move toward the particulars of the factors and the systems that have contributed to this college's success. The "right" pieces we have just described are successful largely because they are tended by administrators, faculty, and staff who want to see the college keep the promises made to its students, to its community, and ultimately, to itself. The factors and systems we describe in the next chapter are institutional responses to those challenges and are totally dependent upon the spirit in which they are implemented. Together, they create systems for success.

4 Working at What Matters: Creating Systems for Student Success

We are bound by the invisible fabrics of interrelated actions.

—Senge et al. 1990

The Community College of Denver has received national recognition for regularly evaluating its own priorities—the activities and programs that it believes matter most for the success of the college. Regional accrediting agencies demand proof of institutional effectiveness in their accreditation requirements. The majority of colleges have written plans for conducting assessments. Yet research indicates few colleges are making the critical linkages between measurable objectives and their mission statements. Survey data show that the first part of the process is done but that data are not collected to complete the process. That is, most community colleges have written mission-linked objectives, but they do not collect appropriate data to inform them if they are achieving these objectives and, therefore, accomplishing their missions (Roueche, Johnson, and Roueche 1997).

The primary obstacle was the low interest of faculty and staff in measuring their colleges' objectives and practices. Most survey respondents observed that the faculty and staff whose collective performance would determine whether the objectives were being achieved did not see the point in collecting the data and thus had little enthusiasm to do so. Second— arguably associated with the problem of lukewarm staff commitment— were the complex issues and challenges of selecting, designing, and implementing appropriate measures to determine how well students were served by the college—in effect, how well students were learning.

What sets the Community College of Denver apart is the college's ability to resolve so many of the problematic issues described by the effectiveness survey respondents. The Community College of Denver today has in place a response system to challenges that, measure for measure, characteristic by characteristic, has not been equaled with proven results. We turn now to the institutional strategies that stand out as the major components of what we have termed CCD's *super-structure*—its systems for student success.

IMPLEMENTING THE ANNUAL PLANNING CYCLE

CCD's annual planning cycle has been named at every level of the college, beginning with the president, as the single most critical component in the institution's superstructure. As the linchpin of the assessment enterprise, this cycle incorporates, addresses, and embraces all the challenges and issues associated with institutional effectiveness. The planning cycle has exceeded all expectations as a collaborative activity and as a successful, albeit risky, venture for the college.

Each year as CCD evaluates its achievements, sets its desired outcomes for the upcoming year, and lists its projections for the following, it produces a plan of action based upon the range of talents, full support, and active participation of the entire CCD family in committing itself to student learning. It is an understatement to say it is simply an extraordinary student success model. The cycle has earned the support and respect of CCD administrators, faculty, and staff over more than a decade of experimentation, implementation, and results.

The cycle does not allow success to signify closure; rather, it continually asks the question: How can this program, or strategy, or initiative be improved to serve all students better? That philosophy and attitude for improved performance are at the very core of student success.

PLANNING AND THE ALLOCATION OF RESOURCES

The annual planning cycle is described best by the array of objectives the college achieves through this process:

- Describe the organization as either developing or deteriorating.

- See an opportunity to create a collective vision of the future.
- Recognize the value in a process of decision making about the future.
- Make best use of resources such as people, money, space, and time.
- Reaffirm values and beliefs under girding the operation of the institution. (Does the budget implement the important values?)
- Stress the necessary interdependence within the organization.
- Identify and address the internal barriers to planning.
- See the potential for resolving conflicts between competing interests.
- Stress a commitment to ongoing internal and external assessment.
- Develop and enforce a plan for planning in a simple format.
- Identify strategic or critical issues through assessment.
- Develop a baseline of information for planning from all sources.
- Focus decision-making efforts on critical issues.
- Schedule research efforts to provide data and information at the appropriate time in the planning cycle.
- Recognize that the credibility of people translating data into useful information is crucial.
- See strategic planning as guiding operational planning (next year) and operational planning as guiding the allocation and reallocation of resources.
- Develop an annual cycle of activity to update the strategic plan, develop the operational plan, and allocate or reallocate resources.
- Involve all levels of the organization in developing the following:
  - Achievements/results of current year (evaluation)
  - Desired outcomes for next year
  - Projections for second year of cycle
- Develop priorities for funding projects based on plans.
- Use plans to decide staffing, equipment, and projects.

FINANCIAL CRISIS

Last year, a declining financial state coupled with increasing demands for services compelled CCD to pay extraordinary attention to maintaining its recognized level of quality service and instruction. Increases in tuition and fees as an operational necessity is painful, especially for students—those who can least afford the additional costs. Moreover, many faculty and staff at CCD remain concerned that it could adversely affect total enrollment. Fewer enrollees means not only less tuition and fees, but also fewer funds from the state, as 75 percent of the proposed state increase is tied to maintaining current enrollment. A newly developed funding formula—incorporating the Indicators of Performance—further clouds how the college can continue to finance services already stretched beyond expectations.

Four of five CCD action priorities for 1999–2000 (#1, 2, 3, and 5) were linked to college finances and one (#4) to implications for a learner-centered culture. The college's 1999–2000 action priorities are:

1. Develop and implement a structural reorganization that improves college efficiency, effectiveness, and quality of service.
2. Increase revenue and enhance resources to better serve students.
3. Create a marketing center to develop and implement a comprehensive marketing plan.
4. Develop a better understanding of what it means to be a learner-centered college.
5. Improve customer service for the diverse students and staff.

While CCD's traditional focus on valuing diversity was not a specific action priority for the 1999–2000 year, ongoing initiatives will secure its primary place in the workings of the college.

EXTERNAL FUNDING

CCD pursues outside funding from diverse entities only if those funds can be used to support priorities, strategies, or initiatives already in place. There must be a match between CCD institutional need and funding objectives before the college will pursue funding. General availability is not a criterion for funding decisions.

Unit plans, developed in response to the action priorities for 1999–2000, are represented by selected objectives in the following list of desirable outcomes. Complete plans specifying how the desirable outcomes are to be achieved are available in the offices of individual units and areas within the college. Some of the priorities listed here have been discussed in Chapters 2 and 3.

COMMUNITY COLLEGE OF DENVER
DESIRABLE OUTCOMES
1999–2000

Goal 1. Reorganization to Improve Efficiency, Effectiveness, and Quality of Service

- The Technical Education Centers system will be fully integrated within Instruction.
- Instructional programs will be realigned to fully integrate courses and programs across all six CCD sites.
- Instruction will be organized into five centers that will operate across the various sites.
- Instruction Team and Student Services will work to create a seamless, holistic advising process leading to a reduction in the number of "undeclared" students.
- New position descriptions will be developed for center deans, campus managers, director, and program/team coordinators.
- The number of vice presidents will be reduced by two and the number of deans by four in the new year.
- Efforts will be made to engage more fully part-time instructors in the life of the institution.
- Student Services will undertake a needs assessment focused on all CCD sites.

Goal 2. Enhance Resources

- Strategic grant will be proposals related to priorities and plans from across the institution.
- The development office will serve as a clearinghouse for all grant proposal activity.
- Efforts will be made to engage Council and Foundation members in collaborative fundraising.
- Health programs will move into state-of-the-art facilities.
- Additional partnerships with business, industry, and community organizations will create new opportunities.

Goal 3. Marketing

- *Inside CCD* and *CCD Wired* will keep all personnel informed about the evolving marketing effort.
- A calendar of public relations efforts and events will be included in the marketing approach.
- Marketing efforts will focus on student recruitment, enrollment, retention, and graduation/transfer.
- A special effort will be focused on all health-related programs.

Goal 4. Learner-Centered College

- Work will continue with the League for Innovation to develop the concept of the learning college.
- Best practices from the La Familia Program will be incorporated into the fabric of the college.
- Revised "Values for Teaching and Learning" and across-the-curriculum efforts will enhance student learning.
- Efforts will be made to expand student opportunities in the scholarship of engagement in learning activities, including a joint effort by Instruction Team and Student Services to enhance cooperative education.
- Team teaching options will be expanded using best practices developed by the faculty.
- The videoconferencing system will be used to deliver programs and services throughout the community partnership network.
- Student Life programs will be examined to ensure that they are all learner-centered.
- *Inside CCD* and *CCD Wired* will have regular stories on the development of a learning college.
- The professional development program will focus on learning, diversity, and technology.

Goal 5. Customer Service for Diverse Students and Staff

- Efforts will be made to enhance the flow of regular and specific feedback to students on their performance.
- The vice president's Council on Diversity will establish goals to align with the Vision [college's vision statement].
- All Student Services staff will attend workshops on customer service.

- Financial Aid will utilize a newsletter and the student newspaper to increase student awareness of issues and deadlines.
- Efforts will be undertaken to establish online registration.
- Information Resources will make institutional research information more readily available to college personnel.
- Career Services will host two Career Fairs.
- Human Resources will complete and implement a revised classification and compensation structure.
- Human Resources will deliver a comprehensive employee orientation program.
- Human Resources will implement a systematic employee recognition and awards program.
- The college will explore the establishment of community learning centers in area high schools.
- The college will explore the establishment of a shuttle service between CCD sites.

Articulating priorities and disseminating action objectives keep the institution's annual budgeting activities focused on CCD's student success perspectives. These activities require a full-team effort to conserve resources and apply them judiciously to support only the programs and activities everyone has agreed upon as the most effective and efficient and, ultimately, most supportive of student success.

BENCHMARKING AND IDENTIFYING BEST PRACTICES

In fall 1998, small teams of three or four faculty, administrators, and directors visited colleges recognized for best practices in programs or strategies in an area of special interest. The teams were also charged with using the collected data to benchmark CCD programs. They also attended a national conference on instructional technology. CCD visited the following institutions:

- Recognition/Rewards—Sinclair Community College, Ohio
- Marketing—Chattanooga State Technical Community College, Tennessee
- Student Retention—William Rainey Harper Community College, Illinois
- Customer Service—Greenville Technical College, South Carolina

- Alternative Resources—St. Petersburg Junior College and Valencia Community College, both in Florida
- Organizational Issues—Santa Barbara City College, California
- Appropriate Uses of and Support for Technology—League for Innovation Technology Conference, Miami, Florida
- Accountability/Data for Decision Making—Midlands Technical College, South Carolina
- Attracting and Retaining a Diverse Mix of Students in the College Community—Seattle Community College District, Washington
- Strategies for Revitalization of Faculty and Staff—Metropolitan Community College, Nebraska
- Communication/Team Building—Lane Community College, Oregon

The individual reports reflected the diversity of the topics and the teams' approach to the tasks. Two of their reports—examining diversity and retention—are included here to exemplify benchmarking activities.

EXAMPLE 1: DIVERSITY TEAM REPORT
SEATTLE COMMUNITY COLLEGE DISTRICT,
SEATTLE, WASHINGTON

Diversity Team Members: [names of members]

I. How the Seattle Community Colleges began their diversity initiatives

Seattle Central Community College began in 1966 in inner-city Seattle and made a tremendous impact on the lives of its students. In 1971, the Seattle Community Colleges began to look seriously at the manner in which the college as a whole managed diversity. They began with the obvious ways of celebrating diversity: with food and costume. For several years, those who chose to celebrate dressed in their cultural costumes and brought traditional foods to share; however, there was a startling awareness that it was the "same" people every year who would opt to celebrate. Also, the faculty and administrators realized that the students were not a part of the celebration as much as they would have liked. They soon realized that this was not an effective way—nor the only way—to celebrate diversity.

In 1984, the college established a diversity committee whose charge was to transform the curriculum and to address issues pertaining to the retention of "students of color." Students of color (Asian, African-American, Hispanic) were enrolling at the college, but their retention rates were miserable. This committee took it upon themselves to get involved beyond the expectations of its mission. They looked at a multicultural model, the Evergreen

Model, that began at the four-year Evergreen State College in Olympia, Washington. This six-week training program was attended by the members of the committee, and they found that the Evergreen Model infused multiculturalism into the curriculum to make sure that multiculturalism was infused into the fabric of the institution. In 1989, the college began experimenting with learning communities with a thematic approach.

After examining the model at Evergreen and after sending teams of faculty/staff administrators to the training sessions, the diversity committee determined that the learning communities were the best formats for multicultural infusion. After 10 years of massaging the ideas, they revised the learning community format to the coordinated studies format that is now part of the required courses for graduation.

II. Issues

1. Resistance from faculty/staff/administrators to diversity committee
2. Retention of students of color
3. Replacing retired faculty with faculty of color to reflect the student population
4. Recruitment of students of color
5. Measuring the outcomes of diversity—collegewide
6. Getting faculty involved in the learning community format
7. Because the learning community format was embraced by predominantly Caucasian faculty, Asian and African-American faculty were very resistant to the learning community format
8. Completion of degrees for students of color

III. Model

The Seattle Community Colleges have a multifaceted model for the implementation of diversity. This model integrates diversity into its: 1) statement of vision and commitment; 2) definition of diversity; 3) recruitment; 4) retention; 5) completion; 6) employment; 7) institutional climate; and 8) learning communities, and this is the model on which our team focused. Learning communities or coordinated studies are the terms used that link existing courses, or restructure curricular material, so students have the opportunities for active learning around specific themes. In addition, faculty members have an opportunity to plan team teaching across disciplinary boundaries. Seattle Central believes that the learning communities present challenges that confront undergraduate education. For example:

1. The need for students to be engaged in more active learning
2. The need for faculty to have greater intellectual interaction with one another
3. The need for less fragmentation and greater coherence for students
4. The need for the college curricula to address issues that cross subject matter boundaries
5. The need for students to explore and understand diverse perspectives
6. The need for creative and low-cost approaches to faculty development

In general, the concept of learning communities is a way of redefining its teaching methods and providing other options for meeting the needs of institutional diversity. Teaching with colleagues and focusing on a theme gives faculty the chance to research a topic of mutual interest, as well as the opportunity to experiment with new approaches to teaching. It is also important to note that strong administrative leadership is critical in order to promote the importance of diversity.

IV. Present diversity

The college developed and implemented diversity-focused programs, hired new staff and faculty, and pushed for the successful adoption of a new Seattle Community College District AA degree program. A comprehensive assessment that included student evaluations of diversity efforts showed that the college's widespread reform efforts paid off. The study demonstrated students have increased their understanding of individuals from different cultures and ethnic backgrounds. In addition, the model successfully promoted faculty revitalization, curricular reform, and inter-institutional articulation.

V. Implications

Resistance from faculty and students was eased through the development of workshops, dinner symposiums, weekly meetings, and various committees. Some of the concerns expressed by faculty and students were anxiety and fear of not being successful, fear of criticism, lack of validation, and apprehension about different approaches of teaching and learning. On the other hand, some possible outcomes were retention rates for students of color equaling or exceeding average college retention rates. Certificates and degree program completion could also meet or exceed the college population. Recruiting, promoting, and hiring faculty of color would help achieve parity with the population of students of color.

EXAMPLE 2: RETENTION TEAM REPORT
WILLIAM RAINEY HARPER COMMUNITY COLLEGE, PALATINE, ILLINOIS

Profile

Team: [members]

Population: 22,000 students, approximately 20 percent full-time, 80 percent part-time

Financial Aid: 13 percent receiving financial aid

Awards: AA, AFA, AES, AAS and 15 certificate programs

Budget: $44,646,544—Full-time faculty 40 percent

Listed below is a brief identification of retention initiatives that the team found to be innovative, creative, and worth exploring by CCD.

Standards of Academic Performance (SOAP) Program

- The Student Development Division designed the Standards of Academic Performance (SOAP) Program as an intrusive advising system.

- Students at risk of being placed on academic probation (with less than a C average) receive a Caution Alert letter after attempting 7 credit hours, and a Warning letter after 16 hours.
- During the warning semester, students complete success contracts which require students to participate in personal and academic intervention strategies.
- Intervention strategies include repetition of courses, career and educational exploration, personal counseling, study skills development, and college motivation.
- Students in probation status are blocked from registering until they have completed success contracts with an advisor. Data are available on the success of this program (see retention task force).

Academic Standards Committee (Subcommittee on Persistence/Retention Strategies)

The Academic Standards Committee is addressing several retention issues and has arrived at the following proposals/pilot studies:

- **Freshman Experience Requirement.** Require participation of full-time degree seeking students in a 4- to 12-hour "learning about the community" course for developmental and for nondevelopmental students and as a freshman-year experience.
- **Developmental Course Work in GPA.** Develop a mechanism by which developmental course work is calculated into the student's GPA for purposes of tracking and inclusion.
- **Prerequisite Assessment Scores in College Courses.** Implement prerequisite assessment scores for college-level courses and a more inclusive assessment requirement for part-time students.
- **Multicultural Education.** Determine a diversity education requirement for students and/or more clearly define diversity courses for students. Continue to offer multicultural educational programs for faculty, staff, and administrators.
- **Early Warning System.** Develop an early warning system to give students feedback by fifth week of semester.
- **Withdrawal Policy.** Develop an administrative withdrawal system which can be activated by faculty. Develop tracking system for students who develop a pattern of withdrawals. Limit the number of hours a student can withdraw without permission.

Research

In addition to the institutional research director, Harper College employs an academic researcher, computer programmer, and two support staff. They provide research data, surveys, and support for instruction and student services for grants, reports, publications, and conference papers. Computer technical support is a separate department.

Orientation

The college has a center for new student orientation. Full-time students participate in a mandatory three-day orientation experience. Part-time students and late registrants attend a two-hour session utilizing an orientation handbook, interactive videos, and trained student orientation leaders.

Challenges

- Parking
- Collaborative partnerships with surrounding businesses
- Meeting the needs of part-time students
- Increasing full-time students
- Working effectively with an increasingly diverse student population and adult students
- Reorganizing as the college adjusts to a new president
- Working with unions as the college reorganizes
- Creating a more cohesive relationship between student services and instruction

Possible Retention Initiatives

- Develop a comprehensive and seamless orientation system that links instruction and student services.
- Gather research on student risk factors and strategies for success/retention.
- Extract best practices from Harper College initiatives to apply and expand retention initiatives.

CCD uses benchmarking to improve its own performance. While there has been no formal effort to link CCD programmatic, strategic, or developmental changes to the benchmarking reports, the data fall into three categories: (1) for designing and implementing responsible change; (2) showing a program, strategy, or initiative is headed in the right direction; and (3) predicting which CCD practices have the greatest likelihood for continuing success.

Assessing Performance Using Quality Indicators

CCD annually reports its performance with guidelines provided by the Colorado Commission of Higher Education (CCHE) performance indicators (including indicators tied to performance funding and those that are not). Each indicator, identified by number and name, are addressed within the following categories: 1. indicator description, 2. operational definition, 3. (proposed) benchmark, 4. source (of reported data), 5. results (at CCD), and 6. conclusion.

The following 21 quality indicators are the major criteria by which CCD evaluates its effectiveness and reports to its constituents and state agencies annually:

1. Student success rate
2. Faculty teaching workload
3. Freshmen retention rate in same institution
4. Career and technical graduates employed or continuing their education
5. Institutional support expenditures per student full-time equivalent (SFTE)
6. Availability of core and required courses
7.

    7.1. Support and success of minority students: minority freshmen retention rate in same institution
    7.2. Minority student success rate

8. Credits required for degree
9. Diversity outcomes
10. Student satisfaction with instruction
11. Academic advising program
12. Results from evaluation of teaching and advising used in employment and salary decision
13. Student evaluations of teaching used in the annual evaluations of faculty
14. Pre-college program involvement
15. Involvement with K–12 educators and principals
16. Graduation year undergraduate assessment program
17. Cooperative education, internships, and service learning opportunities
18. Work force training and/or research devoted to economic development
19. Technology-based learning components in undergraduate courses
20. Internal transfer guides available to students
21. Academic research supported by state funds or tuition includes component impacting teaching and learning

Two sample reports follow. Their simplicity is deceiving and does not prepare the casual reader for the significance of the results statement. However, it is this statement that CCD attends to and by which it monitors its own effectiveness.

SAMPLE REPORT 1

Quality Indicator #4—Career and Technical Graduates Employed or Continuing Their Education

Indicator Description

FY 1998–99 graduates of certificate and associate in applied science degree programs employed or continuing their education during AY 1999–2000.

Operational Definition

Total number of FY 1998–99 graduates of certificate and AAS degree programs = value y. Total number of FY 1998–99 graduates of certificate and AAS degree programs that are employed or continuing their education during AY 1999–2000 = value y.

Benchmark

Value y = 85 percent of value x.

> (Note: Benchmark will be 95 percent, effective AY 2001–02.)

> Source: CCD and Colorado Community College system VE-135 Follow-Up Database

Results

CCD's FY 1998–99 certificate and AAS degree graduate employment and/or continuing education rate is 96.4 percent.

Conclusion

CCD easily exceeds the current 85 percent benchmark on this measure.

However, CCD may have difficulty meeting the proposed 2001–02 benchmark of 95 percent. Graduate placement rates are dependent upon economic conditions, currently excellent.

CCD prides itself on producing quality graduates. CCD was the first Colorado community college to guarantee the competencies of its career and technical education graduates to employers. The high placement rate is indicative of the quality of its graduates.

SAMPLE REPORT 2

Quality Indicator #7.1—Support and Success of Minority Students: Minority Freshmen Retention Rate in Same Institution

Indicator Description

Of the fall 1998 first-time, degree-seeking, minority freshmen students, the percent who reenroll in fall 1999 in the same institution.

Operational Definition

Track the fall 1998 cohort and measure percent who enroll in the same institution in fall 1999.*

Full-time = 12 or more credits taken during fall 1998 semester. Students entering in the preceding summer are included in the cohort if they are full-time in fall.

Benchmark

Expected rate for each institution developed from national comparative institutional data.

Source: CCHE: SURDS [state-level student-unit record-data system] student enrollment (fall 1998 and fall 1999) and degrees granted (FY 1998–1999 and summer 1999) files

Results

As computed by CCHE, CCD's fall 1998 minority freshmen retention rate is 48.7 percent. The Community Colleges of Colorado System staff proposed benchmark for CCD is 46.3 percent based on CCD's 1994 through 1997 average minority freshmen retention rate. CCD's retention rate is slightly above the Colorado community college statewide average of 45.7 percent.

Conclusion

CCD will meet the benchmark for this indicator if the Community Colleges of Colorado System benchmarking proposal is accepted. CCD's minority retention rate has remained relatively flat over the past five years. CCD's minority freshmen retention rate is significantly higher than its retention rate for nonminority freshmen. Given CCD's relatively difficult to serve student population, CCD's minority freshmen retention rate above the statewide community college average is interpreted as validation of our instructional, advising, and retention efforts.

*CCHE has also stated that it will include program graduates, as well as persisters, in the formula numerator.

CCD also evaluates its performance with Unique Performance Indicators, as required by Colorado House Bill 99–229. For the FY 1999–2000 reporting period, CCD reported the following:

Student Satisfaction with Instruction: 50 points

CCD Version: "Report the average rating on a five-point scale for the faculty given by all enrolled students in response to 14 items based on the CCD Values for Teaching and Learning."

CCD Shorthand Version: "Percentage of students expressing satisfaction with instruction."

CCD's every-semester student evaluation of instruction is based on CCD's seven core teaching and learning values. Each student evaluates each course for which she or he is registered. Table 4.1 presents 12,664 student evaluations of instruction for fall 1998 and spring 1999. The overall ratings and individual item ratings are extremely positive and consistent across semesters. Combined semester results show that 95.3 percent of the student overall ratings of instruction were satisfactory or higher. When item means are considered, the highest rated items involve instructor knowledge (#14) and instructor enthusiasm (#9); none of CCD's aspects of instruction are rated low.

Table 4.1 Community College of Denver Student Evaluations of Instruction, 1998–99*

Question	Fall 1998			Spring 1999			Total		
	N	Mean	Percentage Satisfactory or Higher	N	Mean	Percentage Satisfactory or Higher	N	Mean	Percentage Satisfactory or Higher
1. Encourages students to participate in learning activities	6,224	4.20	96.4%	6,413	4.25	97.1%	12,637	4.22	96.8%
2. Challenges students to think/analyze/evaluate	6,230	4.20	96.7%	6,407	4.26	97.5%	12,637	4.23	97.1%
3. Makes the course objectives (goals) clear	6,216	4.05	92.1%	6,399	4.14	94.2%	12,615	4.10	93.2%
4. Is available to students in the lab and/or office	6,135	4.07	94.2%	6,347	4.09	95.0%	12,482	4.08	94.6%
5. Relates subject matter to other classes, programs, life, employment	6,192	4.05	93.7%	6,380	4.11	95.3%	12,572	4.08	94.5%
6. Helps students to become independent learners	6,212	4.10	95.1%	6,394	4.17	96.4%	12,606	4.13	95.8%
7. Returns graded materials in a timely manner	6,194	4.23	95.1%	6,384	4.27	95.7%	12,578	4.25	95.4%
8. Is well organized	6,222	4.19	94.1%	6,407	4.28	95.7%	12,629	4.24	94.9%
9. Is enthusiastic about the subject	6,207	4.36	96.9%	6,387	4.40	97.7%	12,594	4.38	97.3%
10. Clearly explains course requirements	6,208	4.18	93.9%	6,405	4.24	95.4%	12,613	4.21	94.7%
11. Gives useful feedback about students' work and progress	6,198	3.98	91.6%	6,399	4.07	93.0%	12,597	4.03	92.3%
12. Clearly explains course concepts (main ideas)	6,203	4.10	93.1%	6,399	4.19	95.1%	12,602	4.15	94.1%
13. Encourages students to ask questions/express opinions	6,210	4.23	95.1%	6,400	4.30	96.3%	12,610	4.26	95.7%
14. Knows the subject matter	6,050	4.50	97.8%	6,212	4.55	98.3%	12,262	4.52	98.1%
Total	6,237	4.17	94.7%	6,421	4.24	95.9%	12,658	4.20	95.3%

Scoring Key: 5 = Outstanding 4 = Highly Successful 3 = Satisfactory 2 = Needs Improvement 1 = Unsatisfactory

*These evaluations are for Community College of Denver (CCD) classes taught on the Auraria Campus. Although classes at other CCD campuses were evaluated, the data were not entered into a database. Beginning in fall 1999, all classes at all campuses will be included in the database.

Table 4.2 Community College of Denver Diversity Outcomes: Ethnicity of Graduates and Transfers, 1998 and 1999*

Ethnicity	Black	Native American Indian	Asian	Hispanic	Total Minority	White, Non-Hispanic	Total
1997–98							
Number of Graduates	71	16	45	170	302	348	650
Percentage of Graduates	10.9%	2.5%	6.9%	26.2%	46.5%	53.5%	100.0%
Transfers	41	7	45	67	160	163	323
Percentage of Transfers	12.7%	2.2%	13.9%	20.7%	49.5%	50.5%	100.0%
Percentage Available	10.3%	0.8%	2.0%	21.5%	34.8%	65.2%	100.0%
1998–99							
Number of Graduates	68	10	38	151	267	260	527
Percentage of Graduates	12.9%	1.9%	7.2%	28.7%	50.7%	49.3%	100.0%
Number of Transfers	51	7	53	75	186	149	335
Percentage of Transfers	15.2%	2.1%	15.8%	22.4%	55.5%	44.5%	100.0%
Percentage Available	10.3%	0.8%	2.0%	21.5%	34.8%	65.2%	100%

* 'Graduates' data are derived from the Colorado Commission on Higher Education (CCHE) state-level student-unit record-data system (SURDS) FY 1997–98 and FY 1998–99 Degrees Granted Files. Degrees granted data are based on unduplicated, in-state students as formerly used for CCHE affirmative action analyses. Following National Center for Education Statistics guidelines, two nonresident aliens are excluded from the 1998–99 graduate calculations. Data for transfers were provided by CCHE from the SURDS FY 1997–98 and FY 1998–99 Undergraduate Applicant Files. CCD had 380 transfers in FY 1997–98 and 389 in FY 1998–99. The calculations exclude 29 nonresident aliens and 28 transfers of unknown ethnicity in FY 1997–98 and exclude 380 transfers and 26 transfers of unknown ethnicity in 1998–99. The 1990 U.S. Census was the source for service area availability data. Availability data are derived from the Colorado general population age 18 and over.

Diversity Outcomes: 100 points

CCD version: "Report the percent of successful students (graduation and/or transfer) who are people of color compared to the percent of the adult population of the service area who are people of color."

CCC Shorthand Version: "Percentage of successful students (graduation and/or transfer) of color compared to percentage of adult service area who are people of color."

Table 4.2 shows CCD's FY 1998 and FY 1999 graduation and transfer data by ethnicity. For many years, CCD has had the highest portion of minority graduates among Colorado public postsecondary institutions. CCD reached a major milestone this past academic year (1998–99) when more than half (50.7 percent) of our graduates were people of color. CCD's graduate proportion of people of color outstrips adult service area availability for all ethnic "minority" groups.

CCD also has the highest proportion of minority transfer students to Colorado public postsecondary four-year institutions among Colorado's community colleges. CCD reached a second major milestone in academic year 1998–99 when more than half (55.5 percent) of student transfers were people of color. CCD's transfer student proportion of people of color outstrips adult service area availability for all ethnic "minority" groups with the exception of Latinos in 1997–98 when the percentage of Latino transfers was 20.7 percent compared to 21.5 percent service area availability.

CCD has created a climate conducive to setting goals and a tradition of collecting goal-related achievement data and making appropriate changes to improve performance.

MAINTAINING AN AWARD-WINNING TEACHING/LEARNING CENTER

Faculty have opportunities to take advantage of more than 100 seminars each year on an array of topics to improve teaching and learning. In addition, strong applications by faculty for mini-grants will be rewarded with dollars to underwrite exploration or implementation of strategies or initiatives that reflect and support college priorities.

Furthermore, many of these mini-grant recipients are encouraged to share their work with a larger group of interested faculty. From these information-sharing sessions, other opportunities evolve. The T/LC has developed a variety of resources, including annotated bibliographies and reference materials for numerous topical areas such as Web-based research, electronic instruction, diversity issues, course content guidelines, and the like. Each list is updated so faculty can remain on the cutting-edge of new information and best strategies without outlaying limited funds.

BUILDING BRIDGES WITH THE ACADEMIC SUPPORT CENTER

A critical bridge between instruction and student services, the Academic Support Center supports and strengthens classroom, lab, and tutorial initiatives. It houses a multitude of student services, categorized either as lab tutoring or student support. Coordinators and case managers work together to monitor student learning and intervene when academic and/or personal situations change or otherwise warrant their attention. As well, the Academic Support Center offers opportunities for students and faculty alike to receive up-to-date computer instruction to help improve technical skills and become more computer literate (identified at CCD as a sixth basic skill).

Perhaps its most successful strategy—at least to which significant retention data can be linked—is Project Success, the computerized early alert system. Students receive progress letters during the first quarter of the term; they are provided feedback on their progress in each course for which they are enrolled, and appropriate referrals are made to college support services. The services are available on a specific day in which all classes are cancelled in order to give students maximum opportunity to access appropriate services.

IMPLEMENTING A CENTRALIZED DEVELOPMENTAL EDUCATION PROGRAM

The centralized developmental education model works for CCD. All support services are consolidated under a single unit—in this case, the Academic Support Center. This consolidation not only improves cus-tomer service—especially for at-risk students who may find it difficult to identify services for themselves or may be uninformed about potential aid—but it helps coordinate efforts between the array of services.

A mandatory one-hour-minimum lab requirement associated with developmental course work encourages and often promotes students to seek additional hours for tutoring and other skill development activities. Student reports indicate that once involved with tutors and with faculty—in a supportive and helpful environment—their academic performance improves. In addition, many students observe they would not have sought academic help if left on their own. Lab sign-in rosters not only help faculty monitor students' time in the lab but help faculty compile data regarding lab activities and improved student performance.

CCD has the largest number and percentages of its student body in developmental courses and the largest number of multiple developmental course-takers of any community college in Colorado. Students entering CCD with assessment test scores below program entry level in any component of the Computerized Placement Tests are encouraged to enroll in developmental courses. They continue these courses until they achieve competency levels indicating college-level work is attainable.

Placement is not mandatory, but students who choose not to enroll in the basic skills courses must sign a waiver. The waiver states that they have discussed the recommendations and understand that failure to complete the courses may jeopardize their academic progress. Students who elect to take one or two developmental courses may be allowed to enroll in certificate and degree credit classes on the condition these classes do not require the basic skills for which remediation has been recommended.

The keys to success in developmental education at CCD have been identified through program and policy evaluations as:

- Institutional assessment, planning, and budgeting
- Institutional commitment
- Cultural sensitivity
- Entry-level assessment
- Exit competencies
- Computer technology
- Tutors/mentors
- Professional development priority
- Accountability
- Integration of grant-funded efforts

EXPANDING ACADEMIC ADVISING

Key to the success of academic advising is recognizing the critical nature of the undecided and the unprepared student—requiring academic guidance upon entering college. New students complete a computerized self-assessment form, and survey and demographic data are compared to student backgrounds to identify those most at risk of academic failure. Moreover, they are identified on faculty rosters as students who may need tutoring, additional support, or financial aid. Faculty are thus able to identify at-risk students quickly via this "early alert" procedure than is possible with traditional advance information.

In addition, CCD policy requires that students receive structured information about their program and degree choices. In the past, students selected a major program of study based solely on interest. Today, CCD requires that students complete program applications to become familiar with the recommended prerequisite knowledge, the required levels of basic skill development, and other pertinent details. CCD collects data to determine how well students fare in various programs vis-à-vis their pre-enrollment skill and experience levels—valuable information for future academic advising sessions. An advising center was created for students planning to transfer to four-year institutions answering their questions about colleges and upper-level programs of study. All these components— the self-assessment form, faculty roster notations, program applications, and the transfer advising center—form an expanded advising system.

CCD's faculty, staff, and administrators agree that to achieve advising excellence, they must

- Be personally and professionally committed to helping students
- Understand the value of active listening, focusing on students' strengths and potential
- Commit the time and effort to know college policy and practice to provide students with accurate, useful information
- View long-range planning and immediate problem solving as an essential part of effective advising
- Improve both the style and substance of his or her advising role by staying current with the trends in advising, such as continuing education and professional development
- Respect the diverse cultural background of each student at CCD and create a positive advising and communication milieu

Moreover, they agree that CCD's integrated advising system enriches a new student's experience in the college, and they identify the following strategies and programs as particularly successful:

- CCD Welcome Center
- One-stop information, orientation, assessment, advising, pre-admission counseling, and registration
- Referral to educational case management teams within instructional centers
- Student Success Center
- Career and educational program exploration
- Referral to special support student service options and case managers
- Program Success Centers
- Educational case managers, program/team coordinators, faculty advisers, and peer mentors/tutors
- Program-specific advising, educational planning, and enrollment
- Student Smart Start Program
- Intensive staffing and advising during peak periods of registration
- Referral to Student Success Centers

IMPLEMENTING EDUCATIONAL CASE MANAGEMENT TEAMS

Another major contributor to student retention are case management teams. These teams humanize the academic experience by lavishing more time and attention on each student. This model is used at the technical education centers, in the La Familia Scholars Program, and (minimally) within the Academic Support Center. Small groups of students, working with peer mentors, expand the circle of support coordinated by the manager. In focus group discussions, CCD students report case managers work as advocates, problem solvers, and friends to help solve problems with childcare, financial aid, and other personal barriers.

Case managers first meet with students to reassure them about what lies ahead, to assess their basic skills, and then to develop a plan. The plans are as individual as the students—one size does not fit all in this model. The managers map out with each student an approach to a program of study; time limits, structures, and alternative approaches are carefully considered. Student achievement data indicate that the individualized attention paid to matching the details of the students' academic and personal needs significantly increase a student's chance for success.

Using Technology In a High-Tech, High-Touch Climate

CCD scores impressively in computer availability for students. In 1997, a study of computer availability in Colorado's community colleges revealed CCD had a student full-time-equivalency to *institutional* computer ratio of 3.0; the statewide average was 4.4 while the national average was 3.86. The student full-time-equivalency per instructional computer was 3.7 compared with the statewide average of 6.5 and 6.3 nationally.

CCD is similarly impressive in faculty access to computers. In a statewide study, CCD was ranked first in technology training for faculty; recognized as a leader in the availability of multimedia Pentium computers; and identified as having 40 percent more instructional computers than any other community college in the state even though CCD is only the third largest.

CCD uses computer technology to effectively streamline such necessary institutional functions as registration, advisement, and assessment. Yet CCD recognizes the limits of technology as well: Students cannot be well served without interaction—in the form of direction and support—with human beings. CCD seeks to balance the efficiency of technological function with the critical intervention of caring professionals.

For example, in the lab environment, students improve their technological skills as they build academic skills. Expansion efforts add software systems and processes by which students can receive immediate feedback from tutors, learning how well they are performing in math or in writing. The Academic Support Center trains faculty and staff in how to use the instructional technologies.

Moreover, students learn that CCD considers computer literacy a basic skill. Faculty view computer use as a "natural progression" that will force students to integrate computer use with other basic skills to solve problems, perform tasks, and eventually obtain jobs. CCD recognizes keyboarding skills—and computer use overall—as a vital job requirement in today's economy.

Recognizing Faculty

CCD recognizes outstanding faculty and staff performance through many avenues including a "Celebration of Faculty," the "Employee Celebration," and on-the-spot recognitions. Traditionally, in spring, the college dedicates an afternoon to recognizing full- and part-time faculty and staff excellence. While there was only one winner in each category, all nominees were introduced and recognized for their contributions to the college. During this event, attendees have an opportunity to share in the accomplishments of fellow workers, and also to enjoy faculty and staff camaraderie, good food, and interesting door prizes.

In addition to the celebration, a Faculty of the Year newsletter profiling all recipients and nominees is distributed to college employees at every level.

The format was modified for spring 2000. As in the past, the faculty council accepted nominations from across the campus. But following the announcing of the nominees came a new twist: All faculty voted for one full- and one part-time faculty member of the year. The names of the top five full- and part-time faculty recipients were announced at the annual Celebration of Faculty event.

Similarly, CCD administrative, classified, and professional/technical councils also selected employee of the year candidates. Council-selected recipients were announced at an all-college Employee Celebration held late spring, along with the faculty recipients. Other awards were announced at the celebration: "Esprit d'CCD," "Communicator Extraordinaire," "Faculty Advising Excellence," plus presidential awards.

Still under development, the intent of CCD's On-the-Spot Reward Program is to recognize and reward CCD employees who perform extraordinary acts (large or small) supporting goals and objectives of the CCD mission statement and reflecting college action priorities. Unlike many reward programs, this recognition process is meant to be spontaneous and focuses on "individual student success, care for the college family, and connecting with communities." Awards are coupons to sports events, symphonies, musical performances, restaurants, and the like.

IMPLEMENTING A PAY-FOR-PERFORMANCE PLAN

Established to recognize and reward performance, CCD's faculty pay-for-performance plan has not begun as a result of insufficient state funding. However, CCD faculty continue to strive for the highest possible performance ratings knowing that the monetary reward, if any, will be minimal at best in the foreseeable future.

In 1994, after years of formal and informal faculty lobbying, the Colorado General Assembly instructed the State Board for Community Colleges and Occupational Education to submit a plan to resolve the issue of faculty salary inadequacies by year's end. The salary stagnation problem was multifaceted; community colleges had decade-long enrollment increases, received limited state funding, and paid salaries well below those of neighboring states.

In response the state board submitted a proposal increasing faculty salaries for the 1995–96 budget year, and also raising salaries to match regional averages. The proposal also stipulated all two-year colleges would abolish current full-time faculty salary policies and, in the next year, design and implement a new performance-based salary plan. The purpose was to change from the traditional method of promotion based on degree attainment and seniority to a professional contribution and accomplishment basis.

Approved in December 1994, the policy required all state community colleges to submit a professional salary and advancement plan. For buy-in purposes, policy stipulations required faculty involvement throughout the design and implementation process. Although each community college had the opportunity to develop its own plan, each plan had to include procedures addressing initial placement and hiring levels, level advancement, and annual salary adjustments.

CCD administrators and faculty began developing their plan in January 1995 for implementation in October 1995. Papers, forums, and retreats provided an array of opportunities for everyone at the college to have input into the plan's design and implementation strategies. Ultimately, the pay-for-performance model was crafted and ready for implementation. The tone was set for the process by these statements:

> The Community College of Denver's process and standards for faculty appraisal, advancement, and salary adjustment are designed to reward and promote teaching excellence.

> The process and standards are a means of focusing our collective attention on teaching effectiveness, examining our assumptions, and creating a shared academic culture dedicated to continuously improving the equality of instruction at the Community College of Denver.

> The Teaching Faculty Job Description and Annual Performance Appraisal describe expectations for quality teaching that are explicit and public; procedures for

systematically gathering evidence on how well perform-
ance matches those expectations; guidelines for analyz-
ing objectively and quantitatively the available evidence;
and directions for using the resulting information to
document, explain, and improve performance.

The establishment and measurement of both process
and standards for performance appraisal are performed
in a collegial manner and through collaborative
processes.

CCD's pay process specifically addresses the issues of level and salary placement, market demand, and the various level definitions for new hires. Faculty position descriptions are designed to reflect the teaching/learning values and are tied to both performance appraisal and the pay-for-performance processes. In addition, the policy outlines the criteria and procedures for advancement and the annual salary adjustment objectives. The following criteria percentages are used for reviewing and weighing the various portfolio elements:

- 80 percent teaching job/effectiveness
  - student evaluations 50 percent (40 percent of total)
  - dean's classroom observations 25 percent (20 percent of total)
  - personal annual accomplishments 25 percent (20 percent of total)
- 10 percent professional contributions, accomplishments, education, and training
- 10 percent service to CCD (Community College of Denver 1999, 29)

Each employee's annual performance rating affects his or her salary increase, awarded from the CCD's faculty salary pool. The pool is divided into two categories—a performance award pool (40 percent maximum of total pool) and a merit award pool (60 percent maximum of total pool). All faculty rated satisfactory or above qualify for a performance increase. Many faculty will also qualify for merit awards based on performance, advancement, and merit. Funded by non-general funds, merit awards come from one-time sources such as interest, grant, and foundation monies.

Unfortunately, according to the CCD Faculty Pay Plan, this salary distribution model is only activated when pool funding "equals or exceeds 75 percent of the Consumer Price Index as identified in the legislative general fund appropriate process." When the fund fails to meet this percentage, the distribution model is disregarded for that fiscal year and faculty increases are distributed according to an alternative college model included in the pay plan policy.

As the plan was being readied for operation, President McClenney observed:

> *Accountability really begins to mean something when the paycheck and contract renewal rest on the outcome of a performance review process. Development of the policy would not have been possible without all the other "building blocks" and the extensive involvement of faculty and administrators in a very interactive process. The challenge of making the pay-for-performance process work is daunting, but the potential reward is enormous. (1997b, 222)*

Initial responses to the plan produced mixed feelings. Some faculty raised questions about equity of rewards, negative effects of competition, consistency across programs and divisions, and availability of funds to support the program. The college's new pay plan went into effect in June 1996. After a study of the first two years of CCD's faculty pay plan, a visiting researcher reported:

> *Despite significant time pressures, markedly diverse opinions and natural resistance to a potentially threatening change initiative, one of the clearest findings from this study is that the faculty and staff of CCD overcame these challenges to design the pay plan as a tool for introspection, discussion, and accountability aimed at continually improving what faculty do best at the college—serve student learning. (Miles 1996, 2)*

The college has yet to achieve mandate funding in five years of operation and the future of such funding, based on legislative and state board projections, appears bleak. Nevertheless, CCD faculty and deans continue to adhere in spirit to the policy's process and find the process worthwhile.

This fact illustrates the faculty's high level of dedication and commitment to their profession and to their students—indicators worth celebrating.

GUARANTEEING STUDENT LEARNING AND DEGREE TRANSFERABILITY

CCD faculty and staff set about more than a decade ago deciding what graduates of college programs should know and be able to do. They began with occupational (career) programs, established competencies, and offered guarantees to employers that their graduates would possess these competencies. Eventually, competencies were identified for all CCD courses and programs, leading subsequently to guarantees of the transferability of all associate in arts and associate in science courses. Moreover, reviews and revisions of exit competencies are conducted as part of the review cycle for all programs.

Conditions of the job competency guarantee policy include the following:

- The graduate must have an associate in applied science degree from May 1990 or thereafter in an occupational program identified in the college catalog.
- The graduate must have completed the associate in applied science degree at CCD (with a majority of credits earned at CCD) and must have completed the degree within a four-year time span.
- Graduates must be employed full-time in an area directly related to the area of program concentration as certified by the Job Placement Office.
- Employment must commence within 12 months of graduation.
- The employer must certify in writing that the employee is lacking entry-level skills identified by CCD as the employee's program competencies and must specify the areas of deficiency within 90 days of graduate's initial employment.
- The employer, graduate, division dean, job placement counselor, and appropriate faculty member will develop a written plan for retraining.
- Retraining will be limited to nine credit hours related to the identified skill deficiency and to those classes regularly scheduled during the period covered by the retraining plan.
- All retraining must be completed within a calendar year from the time the plan is agreed upon.

- The graduate and/or employer is responsible for the cost of books, insurance, uniforms, fees, and other course-related expenses.
- The guarantee does not imply that the graduate will pass any licensing or qualifying examination for a particular career.
- Student's sole remedy against CCD and its employees for skill deficiencies shall be limited to nine credit hours of tuition-free education under conditions described above.

Eventually, competencies were identified for all CCD courses and programs, leading to guarantees on all associate in arts and associate in science courses. Moreover, revisions of exit competencies are conducted as part of the review cycle for all programs.

RESPONDING TO COMMUNITY NEEDS

As CCD discovered, the Denver community had numerous needs that the college could address. The first decision was to organize a specific outreach initiative to serve the poorest residents of the city by establishing technical education centers in neighborhoods. The residents could access services easily, avoiding transportation costs to campus. The open-entry, open-exit centers offer remedial instruction and one-year certificate programs in career fields. Using the case management model and self-paced instruction—as well as faculty who provide additional lab support along with computer-assisted learning—the technical education centers have given CCD a successful educational presence in the metropolitan area, backed by data to support future funding decisions.

CCD responses to community needs were described in the preceding chapter; of them, perhaps the Denver Education Network is the largest approach to establishing a higher education presence in the metropolitan area. As convener and host, CCD has defined some new roles colleges can play, regardless of precedent, to improve their communities.

A FINAL WORD FROM CCD

At their core, CCD's systems for success are a rich mix of actions based on the profound beliefs of its faculty, administrators, and staff that they can and will affect positively the life of their community. The institution has demonstrated courage in its resolve to disseminate the particulars of its vision—action plans—that the community can understand and, more important, find relevant to its own growth and development. There are significant indications that the college has earned a remarkable level of trust from its community—a mixture of hope and positive expectation.

Looking back, CCD identifies significant milestones to the multiple building blocks essential to creating its vision and its climate for success. Each represents a critical decision from everyone involved, ultimately changing the institution. Together, they are a solid foundation for CCD's potential:

- Exit competencies specified for all programs
- Assessments developed for all competencies
- Assessments incorporated into regular program reviews
- Teaching/Learning Center developed
- Development and integration of six critical skills across the curriculum (reading, computation, writing, computing, speaking/listening, and diversity)
- Development of values for teaching and learning
- Professional development program to reinforce the teaching values
- Classroom observation instruments and student evaluation of instruction modified to reflect values
- Faculty merit pay plan developed with 80 percent of pay based on measured teaching effectiveness

CONCLUSIONS

The Community College of Denver has been recognized nationally, regionally, and statewide for taking bold steps in setting high goals, for evaluating how well these goals are achieved, for measuring institutional effectiveness, for sharing the results of these measurements (outcome data) with internal and external constituents, and for annually raising its standards for itself.

In 1998, before an audience of college leaders, CCD president McClenney identified eight critical questions any college could use to determine if and how well it was delivering on its promises. Today, CCD has a history of answers to these questions, and they mark the pathways of an extraordinary journey.

We end our review of what we learned from this study of CCD's success—success in spite of enormous diversity and extraordinary adversity—with the eight questions its educational leader described as critical to student success. The questions identify multiple guideposts that are important indicators of progress for any college struggling to make good on its own institutional promises in a highly charged context of reduced funding, increasing demands for services, expanding needs of diverse student populations, and challenging institutional goals. The answers must come from individuals who understand and support what it means to be effective at every level of the institution. President McClenney proposed that colleges ask these questions of themselves:

- Do we understand the realities and constraints within which we must work?
- Do we have a way of developing a collective vision of our potential future?
- Do we have a way to identify institutional priorities for a given year?
- Do we properly link plans with the allocation of resources?
- Have we identified our competition and defined our place in the higher education market?
- Do we have processes in place to properly inform and involve constituent groups in planning and budgeting?
- Do we have a way to learn from assessment of outcomes and apply the understandings to alter practices and processes?
- Does our budget implement the important values?

These questions can and will drive change. Deciding to make changes today that have the best chance of making the institution better tomorrow and keeping hope alive in the meantime has been fundamental to the success of this college. CCD has had the courage to look reality in the eye and to see it for what it is—an invitation for the college to do its best.

If the past is prologue, CCD's present achievements will be the architects of positive change in its future and will raise again the standards it sets for itself. Taken to heart, in the interest of informing and improving the academy, CCD's remarkable achievements should raise the standards for everyone.

Making Magic Happen: Implications and Recommendations for the Future

It is [my] major thesis… that the great majority of them, whatever their capability, are short-changed by the system. The principal exceptions would, of course, be those who attend small, private, once-denominational colleges and community colleges, where there is a strong tradition of placing the needs of students rather than the ambitions of professors at the center of the institutions.

—Smith 1990

In the competitive world of economic survival, conventional wisdom would warn us away from explaining magic. After all, institutions and individuals who "work magic" stand out in a predictable, ordinary world.

The power of magic in a competitive environment drives an *exclusive competition*—played out in the tight security measures in high-tech environments, in carefully guarded secret recipes, and the code of silence shared by professional, practicing magicians. But in a collaborative environment, it is an *inclusive competition* that values shared information to improve the common good. The power of magic in this environment attracts the interest of others and serves to inform and improve. In this spirit, building a better mousetrap is an accomplishment of which individuals and institutions can be proud, but the plans for building it do not become trade secrets.

We have learned over time that when the unknown quantity that creates the illusion of magic is explained, we are surprised to learn that the results have been achieved through logical, rational, commonsense approaches to solving problems or creating new situations. Often we ask: "So, why didn't WE think of that?" In all fairness, we also have learned the more amazing the results appear to be, the more likely the approaches were remarkably creative in planning and seriously disciplined in practice. We believe community colleges are capable of such creativity and discipline, that they are capable of being stellar examples of inclusive competitors.

Fortunately for all community colleges, CCD's magic can be explained and it can be reincarnated anywhere—if the creativity and the discipline are dedicated to accomplishing it. President McClenney observed, "If there is any magic in the CCD approach, it is in the tending of the annual cycle of activity." While we believe that President McClenney is correct, we are certain that he modestly understates the case.

Magic pervades the institution—while the cycle provides the impetus where rediscovery and renewal bubble up, it is the multiple facets of the "tending" process—a "shared struggle," according to McClenney—that make the results happen. Fortunately for all community colleges, the CCD magic has faces, personalities, tenacity, presence, and promise. It is a full-team effort fueled by a keen attention on student success, a vested ownership in a shared purpose, a strong pride in work and institution, and a commitment to achieve its collective best. We contend that what has occurred at CCD—and is occurring as we write—has serious implications for all colleges that *choose* to make good on the promise that they have made to the whole of their communities, in general, and to their students, in particular.

We believe it is important to provide some insight into this CCD magic. The findings of this study identify major underpinnings of its foundation and create fertile territory for further discussion. Recommendations address some of the primary issues critical to transforming practices and policies. Taken together, they help describe major ingredients capable of supporting a college of quality and equal opportunity.

IMPLICATIONS

• A COLLEGE'S COMMITMENT TO MAKING GOOD ON THE PROMISE OF THE OPEN DOOR CAN SPUR MANY CHANGES, BUT THE TRANSFORMATION MUST BEGIN WITH THE COLLECTIVE DECISION TO LIVE THE IDEAL OF OPEN DOORS AND ACADEMIC EXCELLENCE.

Aspirations and hopes usually translate into effort, and effort makes something better than what otherwise would have been—for individuals, groups, and the nation.

—Adelman 1992

The transformation of the Community College of Denver began more than a decade ago with a collective decision to uphold the promise of the open door and make this promise a reality in the institution. Although the transformational process has had its painful moments, there is widespread agreement that the extraordinary results were worth every effort. As it was being made, the decision to put all shoulders to the wheel to transform the college may not have appeared to be creative; but in hindsight, it may have been the most important step of all—it was where the magic began.

● **SUCCESSFUL TRANSFORMATIONS REQUIRE COLLEGE LEADERS WHO CAN CHANGE THE VALUES AND BEHAVIORS OF OTHERS IN THE COLLEGE AND FOCUS THE ENTIRE COLLEGE COMMUNITY ON A VISION OF WHAT IT CAN BECOME.**

> *We recognize, I believe, that leadership is interpersonal, that leaders cannot be seen in isolation from followers, that the linkage between the two embraces the dynamics of wants and needs and other motivations, that leadership is largely a teaching process beginning with the parental nurturing of children, that creative leadership is closely related to conflict and crisis or at least to debate and dialogue, and that—above all—transforming leadership carries grave but not always recognized moral implications.*
> —Burns 1978

Commitment to progress and constancy of purpose must be more obvious in the behavior of the college educational leader than in anyone else at the college. CCD president McClenney has established an unwavering commitment to the goal of making good on the promise of the open door, of maximizing second-chance opportunities, and of documenting the remarkable power of education to improve quality of life. He has been committed to these ideas since he began as a young dean of instruction more than three decades ago. No one misunderstands his message or his passion, and he brings others in the college along with a patient hand, respectful of their views and willing to listen.

Research supports the critical nature of *knowledge of self* in effective leadership—that positive self-regard combining a knowledge of one's strengths, the capacity to nurture and develop those strengths, and the ability to discern the fit between one's strengths and the organization's needs (Bennis and Nanus 1985). Moreover, such self-regard extends beyond itself to others, creating in followers a sense of confidence and high expectation. It cultivates interests in functioning at higher levels of performance than anyone thought possible. The results create an atmosphere that is productive and humanly satisfying. It helps create a culture of "shared heart" that can withstand changing times:

> Strong cultures are not only able to respond to an environment, but they also adapt to diverse and changing circumstances. When times are tough, these companies can reach deeply into their shared values and beliefs for the truth and courage to see them through. When new challenges arise, they can adjust.
>
> —Deal and Kennedy 1982, 195

Institutional change is accomplished best by changing the culture of the college, but changing the culture of a college takes extraordinary amounts of time, patience, and determination.

● **A** GRASSROOTS EFFORT AND STRATEGIC INTERDEPENDENCE ARE CRITICAL TO POSITIVE RESULTS: OWNERSHIP OF COLLEGE DECISIONS AND COMMITMENTS TO STUDENT SUCCESS, ACCOMPANIED BY A STRONG AND DELIBERATE WILL TO ACT, ARE CRUCIAL INGREDIENTS FOR HIGH ACHIEVEMENT.

> From my perspective of 24 years as a faculty member at the Community College of Denver (CCD) and more than a decade of service as CCD Faculty Council Chair, it is evident that the current leadership has worked hard to create a collaborative decision-making atmosphere at the college. I have also had the opportunity to compare CCD with other institutions through my role as the faculty representative on the State Board for Colorado Community Colleges and Occupational Education and on the Advisory Council to the Colorado Commission of Higher Education, and I have come to recognize that we have a unique administrative/faculty partnership at CCD.
>
> —Helen Kleysteuber, Professor, Business Technology, Chair, Faculty Council, as cited in O'Banion 1997

"Hard work motivated by a collective vision can produce more positive learning outcomes for students" (McClenney 1997b, 224). Our experience tell us that the linkage—or partnership—between leaders and followers is only as strong as their shared beliefs about the importance of their work together. Hard work and collective vision frame the accomplishments of a long and continuing collaborative process with the ultimate goal of student success.

Allowing the grassroots effort ample time to work, McClenney has demonstrated high levels of trust and confidence in the CCD faculty and staff to identify the college's major action priorities and design the best processes to achieve them. He urged widespread sharing of information and action. Without relinquishing presidential authority, he promoted high levels of institutional buy-in, plan ownership, and faculty and staff commitment. The college is aligned from its mission statement to its individual employee goals, and everyone shares responsibility for the outcomes of the action plans. The president and his top administrators foster a team atmosphere throughout the institution and encourage participation by everyone at every level.

After a study of independent colleges nationwide, researchers reported the operating characteristics of the 10 most "excellent" colleges. One key discriminating characteristic was identified as the *willingness to share information*:

> *The respect for faculty—and the sense of trust that permeates these institutions—is fostered by the sharing of information. Detailed data and the complexities of institutional decisions are communicated in open forums. Faculty are heard on critical issues and know the details when they debate with administrators or among themselves. This depth of faculty understanding mitigates against polarization.*
>
> *—Rice and Austin 1988, 51*

- **COMMITMENT TO SUCCESS REQUIRES AN ENORMOUS CURIOSITY ABOUT IMPROVING PERFORMANCE, AN ENTHUSIASM FOR IDENTIFYING BETTER APPROACHES TO EVERYTHING, AND A PROMISE TO LEAVE BEHIND WHAT NO LONGER WORKS. IT IS A POTENT CATALYST FOR INNOVATION.**

> *Honest criticism is hard to take, particularly from a*
> *relative, a friend, an acquaintance, or a stranger.*
> —*Franklin P. Jones, as cited in McWilliams 1995*

CCD constantly sought out better strategies for improving its perform-ance, and the search was always driven by the idea that until all students were successful, the full measure of making good on the promise has not yet been achieved. It is for this reason, in particular, that many community colleges have embraced a strategy frequently described in continuous quali-ty improvement literature as benchmarking. As a strategy for improving performance by learning from others' successes, benchmarking activities have been cited for making valuable contributions to efforts to increase student retention, improve academic programming, enrich professional development experiences, and expand applications of technology in instruc-tion. However, "[t]oo often . . . the same absence of ethic that constrains continuous improvement makes searching for 'best practices' nonexistent. Most campuses have the ethic, 'we're unique—it won't work here'" (Marchese 1993, 11–12). CCD has been its own measuring stick of best practices as a strategy for raising the bar on itself.

- **COLLEGE INVOLVEMENT WITH THE COMMUNITY HAS THE POTENTIAL OF HIGH RETURN ON EVERY INVESTMENT OF INTEREST, TIME, AND EFFORT.**

> *Parker Palmer is probably right when he says that*
> *"in a healthy society the private and the public are not*
> *mutually exclusive, not in competition with each other.*
> *They are, instead, two halves of a whole, two poles of*
> *a paradox. They work together dialectically, helping to*
> *create and nurture one another."*
> —*Bellah and Associates 1985*

A college's involvement with the community is often an untapped resource. The arguments against colleges expanding their community partnerships or collaboratives swirl around the conglomerate, the mass of activities that can accrue and consume too much of the college's energy. However, Rudyard Kipling's notion that "he travels the fastest who travels alone" no longer applies. A critical balance must be sought between garnering support for college activities from the community and giving to help the community improve its quality of life.

We have documented the challenges facing CCD as budget cuts continue to threaten the array of college services critical to maintaining current levels of student success. With no increases in the traditional sources of funding in the foreseeable future, CCD must continue to expand its pursuit of outside dollars to support programs and initiatives; simultaneously, it must become a presence in the community to encourage increased enrollment. All community colleges are left with two realities: a world shifting toward realizing the interconnections and interdependencies that bind us all, and a need for new partnerships that provide symbiotic support.

RECOMMENDATIONS

• **ASK THE QUESTIONS OF YOUR OWN PERFORMANCE THAT ARE BEING ASKED BY OTHERS AND TAKE ACTION.**
The winds of change in higher education are blowing an array of challenges at community colleges. Arguably among the most serious are two of the primary subjects of this report: demands on current remedial and developmental education programs—already overwhelmed by the numbers of underprepared students and limited funds—to expand their services, and to improve institutional effectiveness with this critical mass continuing in the future.

A compelling new challenge for all Colorado community colleges should hold considerable interest for all others, as well. Colorado House Bill 1464, "Concerning Students Admitted to Institutions of Higher Education," passed in summer 2000. The particulars of this bill—including the far-reaching demands regarding data collection—close up some gaps in the information loop that could generate some new collaborations among public schools and colleges, and certainly provide a database for future research and policy analysis regarding underprepared students.

- **MAKE A COMMITMENT TO QUALITY RESULTS AND SHARE THE EVIDENCE WITH THE LARGER COMMUNITY.**

> *Those organizations that have made quality their*
> *most important goal will live to fight another day.*
> *Those that haven't chosen quality as their goal face*
> *an uncertain future.*
>
> —*Seymour 1993*

In our studies of institutional effectiveness, we have discovered that while colleges individually describe a variety of efforts to achieve quality, collectively they identify the elements by this rather straightforward formula for "causing" it:

- Define what quality means to the market.
- Match market needs with organizational resources, vision, and competitive position.
- Strive to improve quality in areas that create a "quality" advantage.
- Communicate our accomplishments and aspirations to the market. (Seymour 1993, 166)

Whether driven by internal or external demands for quality, or evaluating performance against benchmarks described internally or externally, colleges that talk about effectiveness must be prepared to make good on the future they paint for themselves. Moreover, they must identify the most effective means by which to share their efforts and their results so their constituents will better understand, value, and support those efforts and results. Communicating with the market appears to be the easiest thing to do, but such is not the case. Most colleges do not explain what they do or how well they do it. Some of higher education's history blinds us to alternative ways that we could and should use to tell our story— including traditions about academic freedom insulating us from public view and about the indignity associated with going to the public to convince constituents that what we do is of value and interest.

- **Create an internal unit that regularly discusses, plans, promotes, and supports the improvement of student performance and the celebrations of success.**

> *There is a fascinating convergence in the effective means used to change such U.S. institutions as business, education, family and children services, and health care. From quality circles in business to collaborative decision-making committees in education, people are learning to work together. They are working together because they have to; nothing else works to solve problems or to improve performance.*
>
> *—Chrislip and Larson 1994*

We watched as CCD's annual cycle of planning and resource allocation created multiple opportunities for faculty and administrators to talk about faculty roles and how to identify and measure teaching and learning and institutional excellence. President McClenney referred to this cycle as the "magic" at CCD. It is where it all began, and it has proven to be the glue that holds the institution together in the best and worst of times. It keeps it on track and on course.

Colleges should establish and support strategies that require professionals to enter into meaningful discourse. Administrators, faculty, and staff should talk about their roles and goals—"good talk about good teaching" (Palmer 1993, 8). Even unrelated disciplines have valuable information to share about the life of the college, and beneficial collegial interaction can occur between the most unlikely participants. It is only when everyone understands how each operation contributes to the overall achievement of the college and has a role in assessing how well these activities contribute to overall achievement that the whole will become more than the sum of its parts.

- **Cultivate informal leadership.**

What happens at CCD relies heavily on the ability of individuals and groups within the college to work together for the common good—a lengthy collaborative process. The annual planning cycle began with the president's vision and his ability to pull together all college faculty and staff to establish and achieve important common goals. Subsequent teamwork to tend to the annual cycle requires that each faculty or staff member play a part in the activities most appropriate to his or her programs or job responsibilities. Many CCD faculty and staff observed that different individuals would take the lead on different activities from one meeting to another, that there were multiple opportunities for leadership to change hands or sometimes go totally unnoticed until long after it had been deployed effectively.

Frequent observations of such processes suggest that informal leaders help groups stay on track (Taber 1995): They are, as Max De Pree, former CEO of Herman Miller, observed, the "roving leadership, the indispensable people in our lives who are there when we need them" (Wheatley 1992, 22). The combination—or "confluence of influence" (Taber 1995, 204)—of formal leadership providing the energy, commitment, and foresightedness to start the momentum, and the group members' relying upon and trusting contributions and perspectives of all the stakeholders, is a powerful force in collaborative activities. In her study of the Denver Education Network, Taber observed while her research data did not indicate whether "encountering diversity constructively, confronting conflict openly, and treating one another with care" are requirements for success, she suspected that the shared commitment—or "shared heart"—for the work of this collaborative group significantly increased their chances for successful collaboration (1995, 206).

This study and current research shows that community colleges should provide collaborative skill instruction for faculty and staff—e.g., developing skills to improve their abilities to resolve conflict, form partnerships, and prioritize. Colleges should consider developing their own experts to help resolve group problems, clarify issues, and help others see different points of view.

• HIRE THE BEST AND SUPPORT THEIR WORK.

Quality faculty are critical to student success. CCD takes great care when hiring all faculty, but especially recruiting and hiring quality developmental education faculty. Hiring committees seek individuals who are gifted humanitarians, who understand human needs and deficiencies, and who demonstrate patience and the ability to listen and connect with students. CCD selection committees weed out the gatekeepers, focusing instead on hiring skill-builders who are flexible in their instructional methods and with students. As most of CCD's students must juggle college, work, and family responsibilities, faculty who understand the need for balance in students' personal and academic lives and can help them achieve some measure of it are critical to their success.

In the interview process, applicants must exhibit understanding of their discipline or field; have a thorough knowledge of teaching methods and styles; and know how to relate to students regardless of gender, ethnicity, and background. Regardless of discipline, candidates are instructed to present a lesson plan that best demonstrates their teaching and learning philosophies. In addition, members of the interviewing team present applicants with a student scenario, usually gender or ethnically related, to assess further the philosophical parallels between words and actions.

New faculty hires, both full- and part-time, are indoctrinated in the Teaching/Learning Center and its staff development opportunities. The center conducts an intensive orientation session for all newcomers, and each is assigned a faculty mentor. Mentors are established role models in the college and serve as excellent resources for new faculty learning about the culture of the institution. Not only should colleges recruit and hire the best faculty available, they should proceed to monitor, mentor, and train them in its culture.

• CREATE A CENTRALIZED MODEL FOR DEVELOPMENTAL EDUCATION.

> *People in all areas of college life should be pulling for those involved [in developmental education] since the pipeline needs to supply competent students for all of the other programs.*
>
> *—McClenney 2000*

It is that pivotal point-of-entry at the college where student needs must be assessed and enrollment plans must be weighed prior to making any enrollment decisions. A centralized model, such as CCD's, helps prevent at-risk students from falling through academic cracks in the system and establishes a highly visible presence for the important role that developmental education plays in improving student success at the college.

Although a centralized model works well for CCD, it is essential that colleges considering change conduct a needs assessment and then visit or study successful developmental programs before deciding on the model(s) to adopt or adapt. In cases where decentralization works, there is little reason to consider a change. However, for those colleges contemplating structural changes in the interest of reporting more positive results, this centralized model works. Under any circumstances, an institution's periodic evaluation of its developmental program is essential to determining effectiveness. The most effective and consistently timely evaluation of the developmental experience lies in data reporting the status of past and present developmental students.

- **INTEGRATE TECHNOLOGY INTO THE COLLEGE'S SERVICE AND INSTRUCTIONAL PLANS.** In our fall 2000 *Community College Week* article, "Touched by Technology" (Roueche and Roueche), we identified some of the issues associated with technology's expanding roles in college instruction and service. Emerging and expanding technologies were increasingly familiar sights in classrooms, labs, and students' point-of-entry service areas, according to data from NISOD Teaching Excellence Award recipients, gathered through CCD interviews and publications, and recorded in research documents. Even the most veteran instructors were adapting and adopting technology—requiring students to use computers for completing assignments and collaborating with their peers, thus improving their own classroom presentations and increasing opportunities for communicating with individual students. The most important measure of the effectiveness of instructional technology was the degree to which it expanded or enhanced students' opportunities to improve their achievement levels and, ultimately, to be more successful learners. Unless these were the outcomes, the outlay of funds, time, and effort—typically considerable—simply could not be justified.

Among other recommendations, we urged colleges to make serious efforts toward identifying useful guidelines for minimizing the negative characteristics that are often associated with increased technology— e.g., being isolated from peers or "live" support; being technically uninformed, inexperienced, or poorly trained that drove disinterest or fear; and the like. Moreover, we recommended that they use these guidelines to reduce or eliminate technology's downsides from college services or instructional practices. Data from our current studies indicate that when guidelines are structured around the goal of student success, a common question associated with achieving that goal becomes: How does this practice, strategy, program, or activity affect student learning? Two decades ago, results of a national study of literacy development confirmed that

*Pedagogy cannot be specified independently of
content . . . and content cannot be specified independently
of function or purpose. In other words . . . one cannot
talk about* how *to teach without first talking about* what
is being taught . . . and one cannot talk about what *is
being taught without talking about* why *it is being taught.*

—*Roueche and Comstock 1981, 117–118*

That statement about pedagogy and practice parallels our current
thinking about technology's role in improving teaching and learning. No
longer is the question asked about whether or not technology *should* be
applied to instruction, but rather the questions are *how, how much*, and
to what ends. At CCD, instructional technology is woven into a total
instructional plan. Computer skills are listed permanently with the traditional list of basic skills that should be developed in all courses; among
other basic accomplishments utilizing instructional technologies, all CCD
students should be able to use word processors to prepare their course
assignments, design presentations, and create documents; conduct research
using information on the Internet and college Web sites; collaborate on
assignments; respond to queries from other students and their instructors;
access faculty-prepared packages and assignments; and take exams online.

• SEEK OUTSIDE FUNDING TO SUPPORT COLLEGE INITIATIVES THAT HELP IMPROVE RETENTION AND ACHIEVEMENT.

In comparison to many community colleges, CCD is a relatively poor
institution and struggles constantly to identify funding sources to maintain
programs and strategies. Having faced more than a decade of repeated
cuts in state appropriations, CCD has repeatedly and aggressively sought
outside funding, primarily in the form of grants and special allotments.
Currently, 32 percent of the college revenue depends on grant funding, and
the amount of available grant monies has been seriously reduced over the
last few years. CCD's Office of Institutional Advancement works with all
CCD personnel to seek new funding sources, frequently offering beginning
and advanced grant-writing workshops at all CCD sites with hopes of
expanding the pool of interested grant writers.

There is a concerted effort at CCD to integrate grant-funded efforts:
"Colleges should not miss the opportunity provided by the synergy of
linking all support programs" (McClenney 2000, 4). Faculty and staff
are painfully aware of what reduced funding does to a variety of efforts

to improve retention and achievement, and they are challenged to identify other sources of financial support.

When asked "If you were given three wishes for CCD, what would they be?" President McClenney replied:

> *Money, money, and money. I know money can't buy happiness, but it can buy a lot of education for a lot of people, who then could go out into the community, the state, the nation, and the world and contribute to its quality. Education doesn't have an impact on just one person, but the education of one person has an impact on all of us.*
>
> —*McClenney 1997c, 2*

● **COMMIT TO LEVELING THE EDUCATIONAL PLAYING FIELD.**
CCD takes a strong position for maximizing all opportunities to improve every student's chances for academic success, from assessment and advising, to mentoring and peer collaboration, to financial aid and internships.

Academic advisers are readily available to all students through CCD's Educational Planning and Advising Center, but frequently developmental students seek advising from developmental education faculty. Auraria Campus and technical education centers faculty and staff communicate with each other on a regular basis regarding proper student placement issues. Initially, case managers, advisors, and faculty use a "high-contact" approach to advising students to ensure that they enroll in appropriate levels of course work. This process becomes less rigid over time as students become more successful, and eventually, they take control over their academic decisions. But especially for first-generation college students, this high-contact approach has proven to be beneficial.

Regardless, progress can be short-lived. Columbia University Teachers College President Arthur Levine recently observed: "For poor people, [getting to college] is like buying a lottery ticket. You have to be lucky enough to be noticed" (Macy 2000, 38).

> *In this unprecedented period of economic prosperity, it is time to level the educational playing field. The gap in the college-going rate has actually widened since the late 1970s, when a child from a wealthy family was six times more likely than a child from a poor family to go to college, and when need-based*

financial aid paid a larger proportion of the college
bill. Currently, a privileged child is 10 times more
likely than a poor one to go to college, according to
financial aid policy analyst Tom Mortenson, a Senior
Scholar at the Council for Opportunity in Education.
"In exactly the same way that individuals and fami-
lies have to manage their investments to get the great-
est rate of return, society also has to manage its
investments to get the greatest social return."

—*Macy 2000, 39*

Rounding out its efforts to level the playing field, CCD offers students a culture of valuing diversity, an environment in which students can get the critical help and support they need to achieve their goals. Valuing diversity has never been a hollow goal at CCD; administrators, faculty, and staff point with pride to a college culture that holds student self-esteem, student retention, and student success above all else. Moreover, students talk openly of the empathy and the genuine interest that teachers, mentors, and tutors bring to their personal and classroom relationships, of the extra miles that CCD family members go to remove barriers to student retention—whether the barriers exist inside CCD or outside the college. Many students report that their decisions to remain in college have been made with the support of a kind and caring CCD professional.

CONCLUSIONS

We conclude with an emphasis on the reason the CCD story is compelling. CCD set high goals for itself—it would value the diversity of its students and chart a course by which all students could be successful. But it is especially significant that CCD paid special attention to two goals: to eliminate the differences in outcomes—i.e., persistence from semester-to-semester and to graduation—between students of color and students in the white majority, and students beginning their college work in remedial education and those who did not. While it is not uncommon for colleges to articulate goals for improved student performance, few of them move very far beyond their good intentions. CCD set high goals that would have been remarkable if achieved in any other U.S. community college; the fact that they were achieved in a college with such a diverse student body and such critical shortfalls in funding for instruction and services make them nothing short of magic. But the magic can be explained by persistence and determination, beginning with the decision to make a positive difference in the lives of all CCD students.

Unfortunately, putting CCD's story into print simply cannot do it the justice it deserves. The writing process is limited by time and space, is too flat to bring out the human dimensions that help make it unique, and is too affected by the constancy of rapid change. However, we believed it must be told because the details of the story are important statements about successes achieved in the face of enormous adversities and by determined individuals who have decided to make a difference. CCD has erected valuable signposts along a road toward mission accomplished—making good on the promise of the open door. Such stories are important, necessary, and in demand; they should be told in ways that help others craft similar success.

But even as we close our door on the CCD story, we are reminded of multiple open doors through which the products of this college's efforts pass every day and how powerful their versions of this story will be.

> *A satisfied customer is like a walking billboard.... By exceeding peoples' expectations you make a statement*—their needs come first. *All of us feel good when something like that happens in our lives. It's such a contrast to the every day grind of broken promises, late deliveries, surly secretaries, and unreturned telephone calls. Imagine what would happen if a college... began to exceed the expectations of its customers— employers, students, alumni, parents, board members, state legislators, local community members. Imagine the stories that would be told and retold.*
>
> —Seymour 1993, 179

Community colleges have an important story to tell. If it is a story of life-changing accomplishments and achievements, if it is crafted well, and if it comes alive in the hearts and minds of its students, it will be a story that the public wants to hear.

References

Adelman, C. 1992. *The Way We Are: The Community College as American Thermometer.* Washington, D.C.: U.S. Department of Education.

Alfred, R., et al. 1999. *Core Indicators of Effectiveness for Community Colleges.* 2nd ed. Washington, D.C.: Community College Press, American Association of Community Colleges.

Baker, G. 1998. *Managing Change: A Model for Community College Leaders.* Washington, D.C.: Community College Press, American Association of Community Colleges.

Bellah, R. N., and Associates. 1985. *Habits of the Heart: Individualism and Commitment in American Life.* Berkeley, Calif.: University of California Press.

Bennis, W., and B. Nanus. 1985. *Leaders: The Strategies for Taking Charge.* New York: Harper and Row.

Blanchette, C. M. 1997. *Student Financial Aid: Federal Aid Awarded to Students Taking Remedial Courses* (August) (GAO/HEHS-97-142). Washington D.C.: U.S. General Accounting Office.

Boyer, E. L. 1992. "Curriculum, Culture, and Social Cohesion." *Celebrations* (November).

Boylan, H. R., and W. G. White Jr. 1987. "Educating All the Nation's People: The Historical Roots of Developmental Education, Part I. *Research in Developmental Education* 4 (4): 14. (ERIC Document Reproduction Service No. ED 341 434).

Brier, E. 1984. "Bridging the Academic Preparation Gap: An Historical View." *Journal of Developmental Education* 8 (1): 25.

Brock, W. E. 1993. "Chairman's Preface." In *An American Imperative: Higher Expectations for Higher Education,* The Wingspread Group on Higher Education. Milwaukee, Wis.: The Johnson Foundation.

Brubacher, J. S., and W. Rudy. 1958. *Higher Education in Transition: A History of American Colleges and Universities, 1636–1956.* New York: Harper and Row.

Burns, J. M. 1978. *Leadership.* New York: Harper and Row.

Cardenas, R. 1991. "What the Leaders Are Saying: The Voices of Diversity." In *Underrepresentation and the Question of Diversity: Women and Minorities in the Community College*, R. Gillett-Karam, S. D. Roueche, and J. E. Roueche, 177–206. Washington, D.C.: Community College Press, American Association of Community Colleges.

CCD Facts 1998–99. 1999. Denver: Community College of Denver.

CCD Faculty Handbook: Policies and Procedures. 1999. Denver: The Community College of Denver.

Chrislip, D. D., and C. E. Larson. 1994. *Collaborative Leadership: How Citizens and Civic Leaders Can Make a Difference*. San Francisco: Jossey-Bass.

Cisneros, H. 1996. *Hallmarks of Best Practices in Urban Community Colleges*. Washington, D.C.: Department of Housing and Urban Development.

Cohen, A. M. 1990. "The Case for the Community College." *American Journal of Education* 98 (4) (August): 426–442.

Cross, K. P. 1983. "Can Higher Education Be Equal and Excellent Too? *1982–83 Current Issues in Higher Education* 1: 13. (ERIC Document Reproduction Service No. ED 233 636).

Deal, T. E., and A. A. Kennedy. 1982. *Corporate Cultures: The Rites and Rituals of Corporate Life*. Reading, Mass.: Addison-Wesley.

Drucker, P. 2000. "Putting More Now into Knowledge." *Forbes* (May 15, 2000): 84–94.

Eells, W. C. 1931. *The Junior College*. Boston: Houghton Mifflin.

Ely, E. E. 2000. *Developmental Education in the Learning College*. Unpublished doctoral dissertation. Austin: The University of Texas.

Gillett-Karam, R., S. D. Roueche, and J. E. Roueche. 1991. *Underrepresentation and the Question of Diversity: Women and Minorities in the Community College*. Washington, D.C.: Community College Press, American Association of Community Colleges.

Healy, P. 1998. "CUNY Will Phase Out Remedial Education at Its 4-year Colleges." Internet: http://www.chronicle.com (December 2).

Ignash, J. M. 1997. "Who Should Provide Postsecondary Remedial/Developmental Education?" *New Directions for Community Colleges* 100 (Winter): 5–19.

Jones, H., and H. Richards-Smith. 1987. "Historically Black Colleges and Universities: A Force in Developmental Education, Part II." *Research in Developmental Education* 4 (5): 1–3. (ERIC Document Reproduction Service No. ED 341 434).

Macy, B. 2000."Encouraging the Dream: Lessons Learned from First-Generation College Students." *The College Board Review* 191: 36–40.

Marchese, T. 1993. "TQM: A Time for Ideas." *Change* 25 (May–June): 10–13.

McCabe, R. H. 1982–83. "Quality and the Open-Door Community College." *1982–83 Current Issues in Higher Education* 1: 7–11. (ERIC Document Reproduction Service No. ED 233 636).

McCabe, R. H., and P. R. Day Jr. 1998. *Developmental Education: A Twenty-First Century Social and Economic Imperative*. Mission Viejo, Calif.: League for Innovation in the Community College and The College Board.

McClenney, B. N. 1995. "Community Colleges as a Nexus for Community." In *The Company We Keep: Collaboration in the Community College*, J. E. Roueche, L. S. Taber, and S. D. Roueche, 83–92. Washington, D.C.: Community College Press, American Association of Community Colleges.

———. 1997a. "Productivity and Effectiveness at the Community College of Denver." In *Embracing the Tiger: The Effectiveness Debate and the Community College*, J. E. Roueche, L. F. Johnson, and S. D. Roueche, 71–80. Washington, D.C.: Community College Press, American Association of Community Colleges.

———. 1997b. "The Community College of Denver Creates a Climate for Learning." In *A Learning College for the 21st Century*, T. O'Banion, 211–224. Phoenix: Oryx Press.

———. 1997c. "Q&A with President McClenney: CCD Leadership Sculpts College's Future." *Community College of Denver: The Learning College for the Twenty-First Century*. Denver: Community College of Denver.

———. 2000. "Remediation Is Everyone's Responsibility." *Community College Week* (18 September): 2–3.

McClenney, B. N., and R. M. Flores. 1998. "Community College of Denver Developmental Education." In *Developmental Education: A Twenty-First Century Social and Economic Imperative*, R. H. McCabe and P. R. Day Jr., 45–52. Mission Viejo, Calif.: League for Innovation in the Community College and The College Board.

McClenney, K. M. 1998. "Community Colleges Perched at the Millennium: Perspectives on Innovation, Transformation, and Tomorrow." *Leadership Abstracts* 11 (8).

McClenney, K. M., and B. N. McClenney. 1988. "Managing for Student Success and Institutional Effectiveness." *Community, Technical, and Junior College Journal* 58 (April–May): 53–55.

McWilliams, P. 1995. *The Portable Life 101*. Los Angeles: Prelude Press.

Miles, C. L. 1996. "The Year of the Faculty Pay Plan: A Systems View." *Inside CCD* 10 (18 October): 2.

———. 1997. *Community College Faculty Pay for Performance: A Case Study*. Unpublished doctoral dissertation. Austin: The University of Texas.

Moloney, W. 1996. "Reading at the 8th Grade Level—in College." *Fayetteville Observer-Times* (11 December): 11A.

National Center for Education Statistics (NCES). 1996. *Remedial Education at Higher Education Institutions in Fall 1995.* Washington, D.C.: Office of Educational Research and Improvement, U.S. Department of Education.

North Central Association of Colleges and Schools (NCA). 1993. "Report of a Visit." Report of a visit to Community College of Denver, October 46, 1993, for the Commission of Institutions of Higher Education of the North Central Association of Colleges and Schools.

O'Banion, T. 1997. *A Learning College for the 21st Century.* Phoenix: American Council on Education and The Oryx Press.

―――. 1999. *Launching a Learning-Centered College.* Mission Viejo, Calif.: League for Innovation in the Community College.

Oblinger, D. G., and S. C. Rush, eds. 1997. *The Learning Revolution: The Challenge of Information Technology in the Academy.* Bolton, Mass.: Anker.

Palmer, P. J. 1993. "Good Talk About Good Teaching: Improving Teaching Through Conversation and Community." *Change* 25 (6): 8–13.

Pintozzi, F. 1987. "Developmental Education: Past and Present." Paper developed for Task Force on the Future, School of Education, Kennesaw State College, Marietta, Georgia.

Raisman, N. A. 1994. "Plan for Change before Someone Else Plans It for You. *Trusteeship* 2 (4) (July–August): 23–26.

Reising, B. 1997. "Postsecondary Remediation." *Clearinghouse* 7 (March–April): 172.

Rice, R. E., and A. E. Austin. 1988. "High Faculty Morale: What Exemplary Colleges Do Right." *Change* 20 (2): 51–58.

Roueche, J. E. 1968. *Salvage, Redirection, or Custody? Remedial Education in the Community Junior College.* Washington, D.C.: American Association of Community Colleges.

Roueche, J. E., and G. A. Baker. 1987. *Access and Excellence: The Open-Door College.* Washington, D.C.: The Community College Press, American Association of Community Colleges.

Roueche, J. E., G. A. Baker, and R. Rose. 1989. *Shared Vision: Transformational Leaders in American Community Colleges.* Washington, D.C.: Community College Press, American Association of Community Colleges.

Roueche, J. E., L. F. Johnson, and S. D. Roueche. 1997. *Embracing the Tiger: The Effectiveness Debate and the Community College.* Washington, D.C.: Community College Press, American Association of Community Colleges.

Roueche, J. E., and W. Kirk. 1973. *Catching Up: Remedial Education.* San Francisco: Jossey-Bass.

Roueche, J. E., and S. D. Roueche. 1993. *Between a Rock and a Hard Place: The At-Risk Student in the Open-Door College*. Washington, D.C.: Community College Press, American Association of Community Colleges.

_____. 1999. *High Stakes, High Performance: Making Remedial Education Work*. Washington, D.C.: Community College Press, American Association of Community Colleges.

_____. 2000. "Touched by Technology." *Community College Week* 13 (5).

Roueche, J. E., L. S. Taber, and S. D. Roueche. 1995. *The Company We Keep: Collaboration in the Community College*. Washington, D.C.: Community College Press, American Association of Community Colleges.

Roueche, S. D., and V. N. Comstock. 1981. *A Report on Theory and Method for the Study of Literacy Development in Community Colleges*. Technical Report NIE-400-78-0600. Austin: Program in Community College Education, The University of Texas.

Senge, P. M., et al. 1990. *The Fifth Discipline Fieldbook: Strategies and Tools for Building a Learning Organization*. New York: Doubleday.

Seymour, D. 1993. *On Q: Causing Quality in Higher Education*. Phoenix, Ariz.: American Council on Education and The Oryx Press.

Smith, G. 1998. *Community College of Denver Report on CCD's Response to CCCOES Six Systemwide Quality Indicators and CCHE's Nine Statewide Higher Education Quality Indicators* (September). Denver: The Community College of Denver.

Smith, P. 1990. *Killing the Spirit: Higher Education in America*. New York: Viking.

Taber, L. S. 1995. *The Community College/Community Collaborative: A Case Study*. Unpublished doctoral dissertation. Austin: The University of Texas.

Vaughan, G. B. 1982. *The Community College in America: A Pocket History*. AACJC Pocket Reader 4. Washington, D.C.: American Association of Community and Junior Colleges. (ERIC Document Reproduction Service No. ED 220 140).

Vaughan, G. B., and Associates. 1983. *Issues for Community College Leaders in a New Era*. San Francisco: Jossey-Bass.

Weidner, H. Z. 1990. "Back to the Future." Paper presented at the 41st annual meeting of the Conference on College Composition and Communication, Chicago. (ERIC Document Reproduction Service No. ED 319 045).

Wheatley, M. J. 1992. *Leadership and the New Science: Learning about Organizations from an Orderly Universe*. San Francisco: Berett-Koehler.

Wingspread Group on Higher Education. 1993. *An American Imperative: Higher Expectations for Higher Education*. Racine, Wis.: The Johnson Foundation.

Zwerling, L. S. 1976. *Second Best: The Crisis of the Community College*. New York: McGraw-Hill.

Index

Q

quality results, commitment to, 112

quality standards and indicators, 84–87

R

remedial education. *See* developmental education

resource allocation, planning, 74–75

resources, enhancing, 77

S

Seattle Community College District, 80–82

Service Learning Center (SLC), 58–59

Special Learning Support Program, 52–53

Standards of Academic Performance (SOAP) Program, 82–83

State Board for Community Colleges and Occupational Education (SBCCOE), 26

student performance, improvement of, 113

student satisfaction with instruction, 87, 88

Student Support Services (SSS), 53–55

Summer Bridge Program, 55

supervision, persons responsible for, 38

T

teaching excellence, providing and supporting, 45–65

Teaching/Learning Center (T/LC), 19, 60–61, 115; maintaining an award-winning, 90–91

teaching/learning process, 45

technology: integrating into service and instructional plans, 116–117; using in a high-tech, high-touch climate, 95

transferability of degrees, 100–101

transfers, ethnicity of, 89

TRIO funding, 49

TRIO programs, 53

Truman Commission on Higher Education, 10

tuition and fees, across various cities, 22

tutoring, vocational, 55–56

tutors, 50–51

U

Urban Partnership Project, 66

V

Vocational Tutoring Services (VTS), 55–56

W

workload assignments, persons responsible for, 39

John E. Roueche is a professor and director of the Community College Leadership Program at the University of Texas at Austin. Author of 34 books and more than 150 articles and monographs on educational leadership and teaching effectiveness, Roueche has spoken to more than 1,300 colleges and universities since 1970. He received the 1986 National Leadership Award from the American Association of Community Colleges.

Eileen E. Ely is a recent graduate of the Community College Leadership Program and a senior post-doctoral research fellow at the University of Texas at Austin. She has served on the staffs of Renton Technical College, Washington; Ilisagvik College, Alaska; and, more recently, Iowa Central Community College. She served a semester intern-ship at the Community College of Denver with President Byron McClenney.

Suanne D. Roueche is a senior lecturer in the Department of Educational Administration at the University of Texas at Austin, editor of publications for the National Institute for Staff and Organiza-tional Development, and author of 13 books and more than 40 articles and book chapters. She received the 1997 National Leadership Award from the American Association of Community Colleges.